Walk in the Light

Forgive, Defeat the Enemy and Win

Clare Wilkinson

Heaven Sent

Heaven Sent Publications

Distributed by: New Wine Press, PO Box 17, Chichester, West Sussex.

ISBN: 1 874367 73 6

Typeset by CRB Associates, Reepham, Norfolk
Printed in England by Clays Ltd, St Ives plc.

Acknowledgements

The Lord who has taught me by his Spirit and often through his people, varied and sometimes difficult lessons. Very early on in my Christian walk there was a lady called Peggy, who often said, 'But for the grace of God there go I.'

I pondered on what she said, and the meaning entered my heart. Unknowingly she gave me a right and godly perspective on the human condition.

My thanks for my early teachers to whom I am still grateful for both their sound teaching and their example. Marigold and Nicholas for their encouragement in the 'face of adversity', and example of service. Colin for his courage in adhering to the truth of God's word, his teaching on faith, and for Bob and Ginny.

For Mother's encouragement in the form of many cards and small gifts.

For all at Heaton Baptist Church, both past and present. For the patience and love of those who have listened, prayed and spoken the truth of God's word into my life.

For Judith Black who has faithfully typed all that I have written. Thank you.

For my publisher who encouraged me. It is a demanding process transferring an initial manuscript into completed book form. And for those who designed my book cover.

Thank you.

Contents

Acknowledgements   3

Preface   7

Foreword   9

PART 1: Our Personal Walk   11

Introduction   13

Chapter 1   Starting to Walk in the Light   14

Chapter 2   People's Fear of Light, and Walking in the
             Light   20

Chapter 3   Reasons for, and Encouragement to Walk
             in the Light   25

Chapter 4   The Contrast: Jesus' Love of the Light; the
             Enemy's Hatred of the Light   33

Chapter 5   Walking in the Light Leads to Healthy
             Loving Relationships   42

PART 2: Letting Our Light Shine

47

Chapter 6   Reasons We Find Difficulty in Letting Our
Light Shine

49

Chapter 7   Who We Are, and the Character We
Reflect

58

Chapter 8   The Way in Which We Live

67

Chapter 9   By Our Behaviour

77

Chapter 10   By Our Speech

91

Chapter 11   By Our Actions

102

Chapter 12   The Importance of Letting Our Light
Shine

115

Preface

I have attempted to cover our personal walk with each other in the light, and the victory that this secures us, and our walk in, but not of the world. As the light of this world, our lives should be a testimony and a witness, a light to those in darkness and in Satan's domain, without God and without hope in the world. Our lives can shine a light to those in need, as we learn to let the light of life into our hearts and lives, and as we walk according to God's word, in the light.

Foreword

This book has been written from personal experience. I trust it will give hope to those who have been deceived, who have fallen, or who have been trapped by their sin, and for those feeling down-trodden as if events and circumstances have 'got the better of them'! I pray the Lord will speak to you through the pages of this book.

The devil hates God's people, especially when we walk in truth, in the light. He is a deceiver, a liar and a thief. Jesus gives us the victory and power to change. Even in our daily, seemingly mundane lives, there is a battle to be fought and a victory won. We have a reason and purpose in this dark world. We are the light. Whatever situation or circumstance we walk into, we have the light of life Jesus, the victor, shining in our hearts.

God will defeat those who oppose the truth both in the occurrence of events and circumstances, and the truth of the gospel of light, and those who oppose God's will and God's ways.

I pray we learn to overcome. Walking in the light is a key to securing a right godly victory in our personal lives, and helps us to overcome in this dark world, those who seek to harm and hurt us, and undermine our faith and love of Jesus.

> *'But whoever lives by the truth comes into the light, so that it may be seen plainly that what he has done has been done through God.'* (John 3:21)

Jesus came to destroy the devil's work which is done in darkness, so that we may shine in this world, rising above events and circumstances that would seek to pull us down. May we know the light that is both attractive and life-giving, and show *'the path of the righteous is like the first gleam of dawn, shining ever brighter till the full light of day'* (Proverbs 4:18).

Every blessing

Clare

PART 1

Our Personal Walk

'But if we walk in the light, as he is in the light,
we have fellowship with one another, and the blood of Jesus,
his Son, purifies us from all sin.'

(1 John 1:7)

Introduction

I believe, and have discovered from experience, that walking in the light is a **key** to living in victory over the enemy, and having loving relationships, based on trust. We will be walking in fellowship.[1] *'If we walk in the light, as he is in the light, we have fellowship with one another, and the blood of Jesus, his Son, purifies us from all sin'* (1 John 1:7). Walking in the light is an ongoing process. Jesus said: *'I am the way and the truth and the life.'* (John 14:6). Jesus also said: *'I am the light of the world. Whoever follows me will **never** walk in darkness, but will have the light of life.'* (John 8:12). To follow Jesus we need to walk in the light.

It is so important but such a rare commodity, even among believers, for people to walk in integrity and in the light with each other. Jesus makes it clear that we are not living either in the truth, or in love unless we walk in the light.[2]

References
1. 1 John 1:4–5, 10–11; 2:5–6; Acts 26:17–18
2. 1 John 1:6; 2:6

Chapter 1

Starting to Walk in the Light

Walking in the light is different from walking in the truth. Walking in the light exposes the lies of the enemy. This will gradually lead to people walking in the truth as they reject the lie, and embrace and believe the truth of God's word.[1]

Often our lives are based on lies, or false beliefs, which we do not realize until there is some crisis. Our lives need to be based on a sure foundation; we need to build on rock; the truth of God's word. Jesus is the word made flesh.[2] *'The Word became flesh and made his dwelling among us ... full of grace and truth'* (John 1:14). For example, a person may have a false belief that God does not love them, or they doubt that his dealings with them are loving. Because of the light, a listening person will be able to recognize enemy lies, and point that person to the truth of the many scriptures that speak of God's **unfailing** love for people both in, and outside Jesus.[3] *'God demonstrates his own love for us in this: While we were still sinners, Christ died for us'* (Romans 5:8).[4] *'And we know that in all things God works for the good of those who love him, who have been called according to his purpose'* (Romans 8:28). But if a person does not walk in the light concerning these false beliefs, they will continue to be deceived, and the enemy will undermine their faith. At worst they will blame or hate their Creator. The enemy will have deceived them about both the nature and goodness of Jesus. We are not to let circumstances dictate our beliefs!

The light is important. A person in darkness often will not be able to recognize the enemy 'feeding' him or her lies. (Lies are anything that contradicts the truth of God's word for us, including our feelings.) When our negative feelings, doubts or fears are brought into the light, they can be exposed for what they are; lies, and they **can be replaced** by the truth of God's word. I believe God's word itself is healing, and as we accept God's words for ourselves, healing is initiated.

Walking in the light gives the Lord, by his Holy Spirit, an opportunity to change us. God's Spirit is able to heal the root cause of our personal damage, which may have caused us to continue to latch on to the lies. (They are a false security.) The light unlocks the forgiving, healing work of the cross. We no longer look at our feelings of inadequacy, shame, or useless-ness to dictate who we are or how we behave. As this process continues in our lives, our faith will be brought into line with the truth of who we are, as children of God, revealed in God's word, by his Holy Spirit.

This is often a very painful process as the lies (of the old, sinful nature),[5] have often become so ingrained, working themselves out in our behaviour. We will often need to persist to get the victory – by this I mean, believe, and live in the truth as opposed to being under the lies. When people choose to walk in the light with you, you will need to be very patient and loving with them as they say for the tenth time in floods of tears: 'How can God be working all things together **for** good?'

God's word is creative. God spoke and God created. We can speak God's creative word into people's lives. *'God **said**: "Let there be light," and there was light'* (Genesis 1:3).

*'God **said**: "Let there be an expanse between the waters to separate water from water" ... God called the expanse "sky"'* (Genesis 1:6, 8).

*'God **said**: "Let the water teem with living creatures and let birds fly" ... So God created'* (Genesis 1:20).

All this was created by God's word from something that was formless, empty and dark.[6] Sometimes we feel we are 'noth-ing', 'no good', or, 'useless', because so many false beliefs have been fed us by parents, teachers, the world, and sometimes even the church itself, whose values are often worldly rather than godly. Once these have been recognized, **God's creative word can heal the damage** of spoken lies and create, by the Holy Spirit, a right, healthy self-image. His truth will also grow in us a right God-concept, and a right concept of others. We need then to choose to live our lives with a new identity, in integrity; to walk, talk, think and speak as a child of God.

We walk as one who is in open relationship with God, with no shame, knowing that if we have called upon the name of the Lord Jesus,[7] and have believed in his name, we have been transferred from the kingdom of darkness into the Kingdom of light.[8] And as we walk in the light, the blood of Jesus cleanses us. His forgiveness is continually released for us.

If we want a firm foundation that will stand, we need to start putting God's word into practice. *'Therefore everyone who hears these words of mine and puts them into practice is like a wise man who built his house on a rock'* (Matthew 7:24)[9] The enemy will always try to deceive us and lead us astray, causing us to succumb to temptation and sin. Walking in the light is putting God's word into practice. Walking in the light, and therefore, in fellowship, will help us to recognize and stand more firmly **against** the devil's tactics.[10]

The enemy will always try to prevent someone from walking in the light (he knows the power of God's light). He will try to make us feel isolated or condemned, that no-one will be able to identify with, or be able to help. There are **always** people who know and understand our feelings. *'Praise be to the God and Father of our Lord Jesus Christ, ... who comforts us in all our troubles, so that we can comfort those in any trouble with the comfort we ourselves have received from God'* (2 Corinthians 1:3–4). Because Jesus has identified with us, we can, in him, identify with others. Jesus forgives. The depths of his forgiveness of our faults, failures, misconceptions, and wilful sin, is very deep. As we walk in the light, forgiveness can be spoken into our lives. He will never cast off or push away anyone who comes to him.[11]

The enemy is always seeking to undermine our faith in the

truth and effectiveness of God's word. God's words are Spirit and life. The enemy would also have us accept just some of scripture rejecting the word that might challenge us to change. We may collude with the enemy and **exclude** ourselves by rejecting some of God's word, saying: 'That's not for me, that's too difficult. God does not **really** mean that! or, That's not the way I lead my life.'

We are to submit ourselves to God's authority; his word. *'All scripture is God-breathed and is useful for teaching, rebuking, correcting and training in righteousness'* (2 Timothy 3:16). God's way **is** the right way. It may not agree with our natural thinking or our flesh. But we are to live as God reveals in scripture. When we reject scripture, we reject Jesus.

What does it mean to walk in the light, and how do we start?

Initially we need to get into the Kingdom of light, God's Kingdom. We need to accept, believe and receive Jesus and let his light (Jesus' domain) into our lives.[12] We need to be transferred from the kingdom of darkness (Satan's domain) into the Kingdom of light[13] (Jesus' domain). Jesus said: *'I have come into the world as a light, so that no-one who believes in me should stay in darkness'* (John 12:46).

We need to give all areas of our lives to him, bringing them into the light. It may be helpful to write a list of **all** areas of our life **that we are aware of**, so that we consciously give him, and ask him, to be Lord of every aspect of our lives. Include **positive areas** such as your relationships, home, work, the future, as well as **areas of difficulty and sin**, such as resentment, and fears. These will need forgiveness; and we are to include **people we need to forgive** either for actual, or perceived sin. (It may be beneficial to go through all this with another person.)[14]

After this initial step of walking in the light, it is a continual process of letting the Lord Jesus into more of our lives. There are areas which we need to be aware of, so that God's Holy Spirit, and the light of God's word will reveal:

(a) Sin, and areas of temptation and vulnerability (weakness).

(b) False belief systems (for example, that we can earn our salvation). The entrance of God's **word** brings light and will reveal truth from error.

(c) Our **feelings**, positive emotions as well as hurt and pain, and associated anger. Feelings **can** be deceptive. They need to be expressed. They can be a warning bell. Suppressed feelings cause darkness; attached to them may be unforgiveness.

The reason that walking in the light is a life-long process (hopefully becoming the way we live), is because consciously or unconsciously we all have areas that we have kept hidden from the light. For example, a selfish motive may be revealed in us by the Holy Spirit (we may see, and acknowledge that wrong motive); we then need the desire to change. **This desire will motivate us** to bring that wrong motive into the light, to Jesus, to receive God's forgiveness. The blood of Jesus continuously cleanses us as we walk in the light.

We then ask him to replace that wrong motive with a right, godly heart motive. We may need to ask the Lord Jesus even for the **desire** to change. This desire may increase as we see the harm caused by our selfish motive. We may also need to ask for forgiveness from those we have hurt. **We choose by an act of will to walk with Jesus light**.

Walking in the light may be a painful process in the short-term, but Jesus can turn our sin into an opportunity for his grace.[15] He can turn our failure[16] by his grace, into success. As we walk in the light, Jesus is continually cleansing and purifying us.[17] The more we walk in the light, and **the more of Jesus' forgiveness we can receive**, the more we will reflect his nature.

In accepting the person of Jesus, we need to accept his way. He is Lord, as well as Saviour. If, however, we think we cannot face this pain in the short-term and avoid bringing the issue that God has pointed out, whatever that may be, into the light, God will keep on reminding us of this area. Because God has convicted you, he is in fact asking you to deal with that area; it can no longer stay buried. The fact that you are trying

18

not to hear him on this matter, means that you will fail to hear him on others. This will cloud your open, obedient love relationship with him. Jesus is Lord and will win. Finally, if we are not walking in the light with him, then we can no longer walk in fellowship (open relationship) with others. We affect the Body of Christ. We will neither be walking in truth, or in love.[18] To follow **Jesus** we need to walk in the light.[19]

As we put more of our lives practically into Jesus' hands, his care, we may be surprised to discover what we are like new creations.[20] As Jesus replaces our 'old man', we will see how lovely he can make us, as he cleanses and purifies us from all sin.

References

1. John 17:17
2. 2 John 1:1–7
3. Romans 5:6–8; 8:32; John 3:16; 15:9
4. Isaiah 43:1–4
5. Galatians 2:20; 5:24–25
6. Genesis 1:2
7. Romans 10:13; John 1:12; John 3:18
8. Acts 26:17–18
9. 1 Corinthians 3:10–15; Matthew 7:24–25
10. 2 Corinthians 4:4; Ephesians 5:14
11. John 6:37; Hebrews 10:22–23
12. John 1:12; 3:16–18; Colossians 1:13
13. Acts 26:17–18; Colossians 1:12–13
14. Matthew 18:20
15. Romans 5:20; 8:28; 1 Timothy 1:13–14
16. 1 Corinthians 1:26–31
17. 1 John 1:9
18. 1 John 1:6; 2:10
19. John 8:12
20. 2 Corinthians 5:16–17

Chapter 2

People's Fear of Light, and Walking in the Light

What does it mean to 'walk in darkness?'

Walking in the dark is to hide; to hide our true feelings and motives – negative or positive – to hide our sins or wrong-doing; to hide our failures, faults and weaknesses. Whoever walks in darkness, but says or thinks he is in open, loving relationship with God or others, is not walking in the truth. It is pretending to be what we are not. The person in darkness:

– Causes his brother or sister to stumble.[1]
– Is blind and does not know where he is going. *'He does not know where he is going, because the darkness has blinded him'* (1 John 2:11).

They are neither loving God nor their brother or sister. But, *'Whoever **loves his brother**, lives in the light, and there is nothing in him to make him stumble'* (1 John 2:10).

There are many reasons why people fear to walk in the light and therefore are in darkness:

1. **People cannot face themselves.** We need to ask Jesus for strength to do this. This can sometimes be very painful. We may be ashamed of who we are, and of what we have done.

2. **We cannot face the problems, and issues that will arise that seem unsurmountable.** But remember *'Nothing is impossible with God'* (Luke 1:37).

3. **We believe that others will not accept us, if we are vulnerable and open.** In other words, we fear people's judgements rather than God's, wanting their acceptance **more** than his! *'Fear of man will prove to be a snare, but whoever trusts in the Lord is kept safe'* (Proverbs 29:25). It is better to bring our lives into the light, and hand our difficulties and sin [2] to Jesus, even if it does 'hurt' the pride in us. God wants to deal with that as well!

4. **Simply because our deeds are evil**: *'Everyone who does evil hates the light, and will not come into the light for fear that his deeds will be exposed'* (John 3:20). We do not want to be exposed or purified. But Jesus is waiting to extend his arm of mercy and forgiveness [3] – he has already been punished for that sin.

As long as we are in darkness, sin will remain sin; the darkness will blind us to the truth, deceiving ourselves and others; failure will remain just that, causing us to doubt our position in Christ Jesus and his call on our lives, our consciences will not be clear, [4] and our weakness will still be a target for the enemy.

Reasons why people are prevented from, or fear walking in the light:

1. **People fear rejection, and this may indeed happen.** You may be shut out emotionally or physically because a person is unable, or unwilling, to forgive you. You need to **cling** to the truth of God's word which says that he will never leave you, forsake or fail you. *'Never will I leave you; never will I forsake you'* (Hebrews 13:5)[5] and, he will in no way cast away those who come to him. *'**Whoever** comes to me, I will never drive away'* (John 6:37). As you have walked in the light in obedience, **he** will forgive you.[6] Do not let other people's shortcomings prevent you from having the strength to walk in obedience in the light. *'The stone the builders rejected has become the capstone; the Lord has done this, and it is marvellous in our eyes'* (Matthew 21:42). We need to persevere.

2. **People fear God's condemnation.** This fear is a lie. God's word clearly states: *'There is now no condemnation for*

those who are in Christ Jesus' (Romans 8:1–2). When we condemn ourselves we need to let go of our self-righteousness, and accept the righteousness of Jesus.[7] His blood is enough to cleanse and to cover us.[8] *'If we walk in the light, as he is in the light, we have fellowship with one another, and the blood of Jesus, his Son, purifies us from **all** sin'* (1 John 1:7). The blood of Jesus cleanses us continually as we walk in the light. The truth will set us **free**.[9] The sin, if confessed, can be forgiven and the fears shown to be invalid in the light of God's word. The accusations and feelings of condemnation will be counteracted by God's promise of forgiveness, and because of the **blood** of Jesus, Satan has no grounds or rights to accuse! We will be free from lying accusations, condemnations and self-negating thoughts.

3. **People fear that walking in the light causes more harm than good, or is hurtful**. This questions the goodness of God's word (his commands and instructions), the truth of God's word and God's wisdom. But God's motive is **always** for our good. He is a loving God. His ways are higher than ours. He knows best.[10]

When a person tries to protect someone from knowing the truth, they are believing the lie that to walk in darkness and hide, is better than facing ourselves and our sin. They are allowing that person to run away from him or herself, to run away from God, from reality, and maybe even his or her responsibilities. God's timing is **perfect**.[11] The truth, when it is known, allows us to make informed decisions and choices. If we are given wrong information or lies, we cannot make good, wise or sensible decisions. Jesus always tells the truth.[12] Knowing the truth can lead to a decision for salvation.[13] The truth **saves** people's lives.[14] (It may also cause some to reject Jesus and his way.[15] At least it is an informed decision.)

4. **People are disobedient**. They simply do not want to follow or obey Jesus. There may be an area of sin that they are not willing to give up, but the Lord will not give up either! *'He is patient with you, not wanting anyone to perish, but everyone to come to repentance'* (2 Peter 3:9). This causes a battle between God's will and yours. This can also be an issue, before you

make that initial step for salvation. From then on we need to keep choosing Jesus and his way, whether we feel like it or not! This may cause conflict during our walk, as it deepens with the Lord. Light against darkness. Our flesh-life against a life of walking in the Spirit.

At a certain point in our walk, we may be tempted to sin and go our own way. We need to bring this **'battle area' of temptation into the light** and stand together with other believers against the enemy's tactics to draw us away from Jesus, and his love. We may fail, grieving the Lord, and go our own way. Then we need to repent and Jesus will forgive us, and draw us to himself again. Or we may have been deceived and gone our own way unknowingly, but when the Holy Spirit reveals this to us, we again have to choose to repent. Wilful disobedience removes God's hand of blessing.

5. **A punitive upbringing can cause a person to fear harsh punishment if they walk in the light.** These fears can be overcome, and healed by Jesus. Jesus will always be there, always be with you. He accepts us with our faults and failures, forgives us as we walk in the light. He will lead you, as you ask,[16] to people who are trying to walk as he walked, who are learning to be accepting, forgiving, and non-judgemental. A Christian counsellor should at least have these qualities and be able to direct a person to Jesus, who does accept and forgive[17] your sins, faults and failings. Jesus is a great encourager. He will commend and encourage you,[18] not put you down. God's word says: *'But if we walk in the light, as he is in the light, we have fellowship with one another, and the blood of Jesus, his Son, purifies us from all sin'* (1 John 1:7).

6. **People deprived of the truth, justice and mercy will neither see the sense of walking in the light, nor will they have an expectation of forgiveness for wrongs.** They may have either not been believed, or punished for being truthful. They will be used to punishment for wrongs, faults, and failings, instead of forgiveness and acceptance.

It is good that overcomes evil:[19] the light that overcomes the dark. That person will therefore sadly try to hide his sin, and him or herself from the light, love, forgiveness and healing of Jesus. **Jesus does not hold our sins or count our sins against us.** He freely forgives. Although I do believe repentance means making amends as far as it is possible.[20] Walking in the light is totally contrary to the 'old man' and that belief system. There is such freedom in being known for who we are, and still being accepted. Whatever you have done, **he knows.** He still wants you to start walking in the light with others, to be really known and to receive real acceptance.[21] He loves you. As you begin to do this, you will begin to know abundant life; life in all its fullness.[22]

References

1. 1 John 2:10
2. 1 John 1:9
3. Romans 5:6–10; Ephesians 2:4–5; John 6:37
4. Hebrews 9:14
5. Deuteronomy 31:6, 8; Joshua 1:5
6. 1 John 1:7, 9
7. 1 Corinthians 1:30; 2 Corinthians 5:21; Matthew 9:12–13; Romans 4:23–25
8. 1 Peter 1:18–19; 1 John 1:9
9. John 8:31–32
10. Isaiah 55:8–11
11. Psalm 18:30
12. John 8:31–32, 34; 17:17
13. Romans 10:14–18; John 12:50
14. Proverbs 14:25
15. John 12:48
16. John 14:13–14; 16:24
17. Ephesians 1:7; Psalm 103:12; 1 John 1:9; 1 Corinthians 15:3–4
18. 2 Corinthians 1:3–4; 1 John 2:1–2
19. Romans 12:17, 21; 1 Peter 3:9
20. Luke 19:8; Matthew 3:8; Proverbs 14:9
21. 1 John 1:5–6, 9; Ephesians 1:4
22. John 10:10

Chapter 3

Reasons for, and Encouragement to Walk in the Light

Factors that will help and encourage you to walk in the light:

1. **A strong relationship with Jesus**; knowing his unfailing love. *'All the ways of the Lord are loving and faithful for those who keep the demands of his covenant'* (Psalm 25:10).[1] He may stretch our faith; he may discipline [2] us; but he will **never** let us down. He is totally worthy of trust (it will happen just as he says).[3] We need to be secure in our relationship with the Lord.

2. **Other people's obedience**; people who are already walking, in obedience, in the light. Often other people teach us, by example, to trust Jesus. They are trustworthy themselves. They are like Jesus to us. They have earned our trust by always 'being there when we need them.' They are not condemning all our faults, failings, weaknesses or sin. Their lives are under the guidance of the Holy Spirit. They are, and have submitted, themselves to God. It is a good way to start to ask Jesus to bring a person, a God-given counsellor, or friend, alongside you. This may be during a particularly difficult time, when you need someone special to walk in the light with you.

3. **Knowing God rewards obedience**. Often as people we need to know there will be a positive outcome, a reward, to give us an incentive. Jesus often said that it would not be easy to follow him, but that if people did go his way, there would

be a reward.[4] The desire for a reward; a positive outcome is not self-ambition. We need an incentive, a goal to keep our hope alive, so that we keep on, and persevere in obedience.[5]

As we walk in the light we know:

(a) our sins will be forgiven.[6] *'But if we walk in the light, as he is in the light, we have fellowship with one another, and the blood of Jesus, his Son, purifies us from all sin'* (1 John 1:7);

(b) accompanied by the prayer of a righteous man, we will be healed;[7];

(c) we will have the knowledge of his presence.[8] His presence will be real for us;

(d) we will have confidence before God because our hearts will not condemn us.[9] We know we are pleasing God.

There are also many general rewards for walking in obedience. Our obedience leads to righteousness (Romans 6:16). Walking in the light is an important area of walking in obedience. as Jesus walked.[10] Some of the most wonderful rewards of walking in the light, in obedience, are:

(a) we will have the knowledge of God's love for us.[11] We will have a knowledge of and experience God's love for us;

(b) we will receive what we ask for, if we obey his commands;[12]

(c) we will be **blessed**;[13] in **all** we put our hands to we will prosper. We may suffer for doing what is right, but even then we are **blessed**.[14] We secure our eternal reward, a place in eternity (1 John 2:17), by our obedience.

4. **The foreknowledge that people may well oppose you** for walking in the truth, and the light. This is because they, themselves, are being exposed. If we share in his sufferings, we will **also** share in his glory.[15] People will hate you for exposing them, if their deeds are evil.[16] We must put on the full armour of God.[17] The person who has been exposed has a choice to either: walk in the light, and the blood of Jesus will also cleanse him or her; or, they can choose to continue to walk in darkness and disobedience, to deny the truth and oppose God. God's hand will be against them, but for us [18] who are in the light.

A very difficult area of walking in the light, is when it exposes another person. The person being exposed may deny the reality of the event and the sin they committed; for example, sexual abuse. It is their choice to continue to walk in the darkness.

The counsellor-friend of the abused person, with whom they have walked in the light, then has to decide who to believe: the counselled person or the exposed/accused person. I say it is the counsellor's duty to be on the side of, and to believe and **stand with his or her counsellee**. Even if this is very costly, remember that God is able to forgive and save completely that which is entrusted to him.

It is so destructive for someone who has risked walking in the light to not be believed. It is denying who they are concerning an actual event. It is making them out to be a liar. If we ourselves are in the light; we will be more correctly discerning.

5. **Walking in the light breaks the enemy's hold over us, with prayer, in that area of our lives, giving us freedom**. In many areas of our lives we can choose to walk in the light, facing issues, problems, difficulties and sin, or to walk in darkness and continue to be defeated in those areas. The enemy uses those areas of darkness to keep us in bondage. The light will expose sin, fears, false accusations and condemnation, as well as false or wrong beliefs, all of which the enemy uses to 'trip' us up.[19]

6. **The knowledge, that walking in the light, brings victory over our enemies**. Only in the darkness, can the enemy continue to deceive and attempt to destroy. Negative thought patterns can lead to sin and destructive behaviour. These thought patterns in the light, with prayer by the power of the Holy Spirit, can be broken. We will know we are loved for who we are, and not who we pretend to be (that's a freedom in itself). We will walk more like sons and daughters of the living God.

7. **The knowledge that Jesus can bring us through** every and any situation[20] that we bring into the light to him. God is able. Jesus wants to be included even in the darkest place.

He knows the journey from hell to heaven. He paid for you to be with him, seated in heavenly places. He will guide you, in the light of his word, by his Holy Spirit. He knows the way and how to get us through every situation. We are not to let the enemy deceive us into thinking there is no hope.

8.   **Jesus wants us to shine, to give him glory.**[21] Jesus is able to change us as we walk in the light, so we can reflect his glory.[22] This will attract people who are hungry for Jesus, and in need of his forgiveness. We will reflect what they are searching for. Jesus can make us and others beautiful, as we let the light of Jesus into our lives. Jesus can touch, change, and heal our lives, however marred or scarred, and make us like him. His desire is to lift **us up**.

There are many reasons to help motivate and encourage us to walk according to God's word, in the light.

Reasons for walking in the light:

1.   **Jesus will continually purify and forgive us.**[23] We will be healed.[24] There may be an **underlying hurt causing an area of weakness**, which makes us vulnerable to sin. Jesus wants to heal us so we can live in freedom and victory. It is always good to pray through these areas of our lives, in the light, with Jesus. If the enemy can cause us to sin, he will **rob us** of our joy, our peace, our love relationship with God and other people, and our victorious walk. This negative process can be reversed by the light.

2.   **We will be able to walk with confidence before God and others because our conscience will be clear.**[25] What confidence we will have, and what freedom. The enemy will not be able to undermine our standing in Jesus, or our position and God-given authority as brothers and sisters.[26]

3.   **The light will help us to discern rightly what is of God, and what is of the enemy**. The light exposes the enemy for who he is, and the destructive work he is attempting to do.[27] The devil is the enemy, he is the deceiver, murderer and liar.[28] He is aiming, by lies, to keep people in bondage, sickness, sadness and ultimately, to keep them out of the Kingdom of heaven. If we have been deceived, and in so doing

have made wrong choices, the light will enable us to correct our error, by repentance. We can again walk before the Lord in obedience, and continue to do so, by making the right choices.

4. **The light also shows who God is, and what his nature is**. He is merciful, forgiving, gracious and generous. He is also the truth; that is his intrinsic nature.[29] He cannot lie. God's word reveals the seriousness of lying and deceiving others. Lying is serious in God's eyes. *'The Lord detests lying lips'* (Proverbs 12:22), especially as a believer, because Jesus is: *'The way and the truth and the life'* (John 14:6). Neither are we to listen to lies.[30] We are just doing the devil's work when we speak or listen to lies. God's word clearly states that liars will not inherit the Kingdom of God.[31] *'A false witness will not go unpunished and he who pours out lies will not go free'* (Proverbs 19:5) (unless this sin, as with others, is confessed and repented of). Jesus says we are to speak the truth in love, to build others up.[32] The Lord delights in men who are truthful.

There is **no** point,in hiding, or trying to deceive others – Jesus knows![33] Jesus is not willing that anyone should perish.[34] But it is our choice whether to live in the truth and walk in our inheritance, or to walk falsely (knowingly walking in lies or deceit). God is **good**. His love and his ability are great enough to meet us at our point of need, and forgive us, and lead us through to a place of victory.[35] His desire is for us to win over darkness, deceit, and lies.

5. **Walking in the light will enable us to acknowledge more who Jesus is, and in so doing we will live more in the truth for him**. We will walk increasing in the truth and in reality, getting the Lord's perspective on our lives and difficult situations. The Holy Spirit will be able to guide us into all truth.

6. **Walking in the light will help us to avoid deception**. The heart can be deceptive,[36] the light will help expose self-deception. We can deceive ourselves, especially in the area of our heart motive. The psalmist wisely asks that his hidden faults will be forgiven. The more we walk in the light and let Jesus in, the less likely we are to be deceived. It will also help us to be more discerning in our dealings with others. Jesus was

very honest in his dealings with his heavenly Father, himself and others. Before he went to the cross, he did not deceive himself that that was what he wanted or even what he would naturally choose!

Although his feelings were contrary, he chose to do the right thing nevertheless: *'May your will be done'* (Matthew 26:42). He did so *'for the joy set before him'* (Hebrews 12:2). We need to be honest about the continuous battle that is being fought between choosing God's way, or our way. At times like that, it is important to **bring the area of conflict into God's light**, to help us get the victory, by prayer. We can then ask God to enable us to go his way with a **willing** spirit.

7. **We will be blessed for our obedience.**[37] We may suffer for doing what is right and walking in the light. We are still blessed,[38] for being obedient **he** will honour us. This happens because we make others feel uncomfortable. The light in our lives will **show things as they really are.**[39]

8. **We will be known**. We will have no fear of people discovering what we are really like, and then, possibly being rejected because we pretended to be someone we are not. Wilful deception is serious in God's eyes.[40] It is the enemy's 'work'. Deception is very manipulative. **It gives the deceiving person, a wrong control**. Deception also really hurts people, leading them astray. This can be wilful hurt. It means you either do not want to be known and loved by the person you are deceiving, or you do not trust them to know you. They are self-seeking.

Jesus knows **us**.[41] We cannot hide from him. Jesus understands the fear[42] connected with being known for who we are. This may be especially difficult if we have experienced a deep hurt, or rejection. As you risk walking God's way, in the light, he will go all the way with you. As you begin to trust the Lord Jesus, you will know his unconditional love and acceptance, his dependability.

9. **We will get the victory over the enemy**. As we walk in the light, the blood of Jesus cleanses us from **all** sin.[43] There will be **no** grounds for condemnation or accusation. You will

know more **your rightful standing** before God. This affects our thinking and resultant behaviour.

If the enemy, at some point, has gained access and taken ground due to perpetual sin (ours, or other people's sin against us), that ground can be claimed back. Once the ground has been claimed back by repentance, and we are cleansed by the blood of Jesus, we walk in the light. The demonic strongholds that may have resulted can be dealt with by prayer, thus breaking any demonic hold.[44]

References

1. Hebrews 13:8; Jeremiah 31:3; Psalm 25:10; Isaiah 43:1–4
2. Hebrews 12:7, 11
3. Titus 1:2; Hebrews 6:18
4. Matthew 19:29; Psalm 19:11; Hebrews 10:35–36; Proverbs 3:1–2
5. 1 Peter 1:3–4, 9; Philippians 1:6; 2 Corinthians 1:21–22
6. 1 John 1:9
7. James 5:16
8. Psalm 16:11; 89:15
9. 1 John 3:20–22
10. 1 John 2:5–6, 10
11. John 14:21; 15:10; 1 John 2:5
12. 1 John 3:22–24
13. Deuteronomy 28:1–14; Proverbs 3:1–2
14. 1 Peter 3:14–15; Matthew 5:11
15. Romans 8:17
16. John 3:20; Ephesians 5:11–14
17. Ephesians 6:11–18
18. Isaiah 54:17; 1 Peter 3:12
19. Hebrews 12:1
20. Isaiah 43:1–4; Hebrews 4:14
21. Matthew 5:14–16; Mark 4:21–23
22. 2 Corinthians 3:18
23. 1 John 1:6–7, 9
24. James 5:16; Matthew 18:19–20
25. 1 John 2:10; 3:21–22
26. Hebrews 2:11
27. John 3:19–20; Matthew 10:26–28; Hebrews 4:13
28. John 8:44; 10:10
29. Titus 1:2; John 14:6; Hebrews 6:18
30. John 8:44; Proverbs 6:16–17, 19
31. Revelation 21:8
32. Ephesians 4:15–16
33. Matthew 10:26; Hebrews 4:13
34. John 3:17–18
35. Romans 8:31
36. Psalm 19:12–13; Jeremiah 17:9–10

37. Deuteronomy 28:1–14; 1 John 2:5–6; John 14:21
38. 1 Peter 3:14
39. John 3:20
40. Proverbs 14:5; 19:5; 24:28; 2 Timothy 3:13
41. Psalm 139:1–3; John 10:3; 2 Timothy 2:19
42. Hebrews 2:14, 17–18; 4:15–16
43. 1 John 1:7
44. Matthew 18:19–20

Chapter 4

The Contrast: Jesus' Love of Light; the Enemy's Hatred of the Light

Why does Jesus love the light?

When we love someone, we desire to emulate them, so knowing why Jesus loves the light will both encourage us, and give us a reason to walk as Jesus walked.

1.   **Jesus is the light of the world that gives life.** *'I am the light of the world. Whoever follows me will never walk in darkness, but will have the light of life'* (John 8:12).[1] Light is good, and walking in the light is good. Jesus loves the truth to be known.

2.   **The light will make plain what is done through God.**[2] *'But whoever lives by the truth comes into the light, so that it may be seen plainly that what he has done has been done through God'* (John 3:21). We will be less vulnerable to deception. We will **have** a right God-concept, we will know his nature. We will recognize him. We will learn more about Jesus, his ways, and his dealings with us. We will also help others to avoid being deceived.

3.   **Our desire to know and follow Jesus, and to spend time with him, will increase, as we know him as he really is**.

4.   **We will know the truth and so experience his unconditional love and forgiveness.** It is by **grace** we are saved.[3] We cannot buy or earn God's forgiveness and salvation. They are free gifts[4] to be accepted and cherished. Neither can we manipulate his favour. Jesus is our righteousness.[5] This will

be the end of selfish ambition and self-promotion, and their destructive effects.[6]

5. Walking in the light is redemptive. You choose to turn from Satan and darkness, to God and his light.[7] You will be changed by grace, as you give him the sin, negatives, wrong attitudes, thought patterns and sinful heart motives. These will be replaced by Jesus, as we ask for **his** forgiveness and cleansing, and ask him to change us, by his Holy Spirit. This is an ongoing process.[8]

6. The light breaks wrong behaviour patterns. Here are some examples of behaviour patterns that can be broken:

(a) **Ungodly anger** – possibly against siblings, or a marriage partner. This may be broken immediately, if we are aware and have insight into the reason for our anger. The ungodly anger may not be broken immediately. You may need to **look at the underlying causes** such as unforgiveness, bitterness, or a deep hurt. You then have to choose to walk in the light concerning the root cause, and to forgive and pray through the area, or areas of difficulty, thus breaking the pattern of ungodly anger. The reason for anger could be that we are simply walking in the flesh, gratifying our flesh as opposed to walking by the Spirit. God has given us a spirit of self-control. A fruit of God's Holy Spirit is self-control.

(b) **Adultery** – this is a difficult area to walk in the light with, as it involves another person. Your heart motive needs to be sincere. Jesus **can** get the victory in this area. Sin leads to death. You need to choose, by an act of your will, to overcome in this area and persevere even if you are tempted.[9] *'He who conceals his sins does not prosper, but whoever confesses and renounces them finds mercy'* (Proverbs 28:13). We need to repent. It is the devil who tempts and trips up the saints. Do not do the devil's work by condemning that person.

(c) **Criticism** – walking in the light may reveal a low self-worth, a poor self-image, causing critical behaviour. This pattern can be broken, as you are built up in the truth of God's word. Jesus **always** builds people up.[10]

7. God wants you to know that his word works when we put it into practice.[11] Jesus speaks the truth.[12] God's word is the plumbline against which our thoughts and actions can be measured. So, if God says: *'And we know that in all things God works for the good of those who love him who have been called according to his purpose'* (Romans 8:28), and you are saying the opposite, who is right? **Jesus!** Some people say, 'I will believe if I see;' I say, 'believe and you **will** see.' We are called to walk by **faith.** Our walk is a walk of **faith.** Jesus is able to sympathize with our struggles to believe from the heart, and he will give us more faith as we turn to him and pray for more.[13]

8. Jesus will be able to help us at our point of need[14] **because we will be letting him into the situation.** He loves us walking in the light; this allows him in to help us. If we hide and pretend we have no need, he is unable to help, until we let him into that area. **All** your problems and mine were solved in Jesus on the cross. He 'found' the way from hell to heaven. He became sin for us so we might become the righteousness of God. We are to enter into the finished work of the cross, by grace and faith. He **can** bring us through from hell to heaven.

9. We will be cleansed from the inside. God desires truth on the inside;[15] in our innermost being. Walking in the light purifies us from all sin.[16] We will become clean on the inside as we confess and repent;[17] not open to the charge of being whitewashed tombs and hypocrites.[18]

10. We will be in right relationship with other believers.[19] God says it is **when we walk in fellowship in the light, that we are loving our brothers.**[20] It is such a challenge to walk in the light with others (not just in counselling and ministering situations). We need his help and his grace to enable us.[21]

11. It brings salvation. Jesus sometimes forces people into the light in the hope that they will repent and be saved.[22] If we do not repent, he **will** discipline us.

It clearly states in the scripture that the sexually immoral, along with the idolators, adulterers, prostitutes, homosexuals, thieves, the greedy, slanderers and swindlers, will not inherit the Kingdom of God.[23] In Corinthians, and in many other places in scripture, God's word shows us that God has made provision for people who have sinned in this way, to be forgiven and saved.[24] Jesus is able to save completely that which is entrusted to him [25] by his blood, and because of the **finished work** of the cross.[26] The wages of sin is death; the gift of God is eternal life through our Lord Jesus Christ.[27] Scripture clearly states that we, as believers, are **not** to associate with someone who calls himself our brother but who is sexually immoral.[28]

If that person does not acknowledge his sin and repent, he is to be handed over to Satan. Why?

(a) so the **sinful nature** (not the man or woman) may be destroyed and the **spirit saved** on the day of Christ.[29] *'Expel the wicked man from among you.'*[30] Why?

(b) because a small amount of wickedness spreads – a little bit of mud in a clear glass of water can dirty the whole glassful. *'Don't you know that a little yeast works through the whole batch of dough?'*[31]

The Lord Jesus is trying to protect us from falling, from being led astray, from putting our own salvation at risk. He yearns for us. Our bodies belong to the Lord. We are a *'royal priesthood, a holy nation, a people belonging to God that you may declare the praises of him who called you out of darkness into his wonderful light'* (1 Peter 2:9)[32]

There is a clear distinction in God's expectation between those who are of the world, those who have never known Jesus, and those who belong to him.[33] *'No-one who lives in him keeps on sinning'* (1 John 3:6). *'No-one who is born of God will continue to sin'* (1 John 3:9).[34] We no longer live according to the sinful nature but according to the Spirit.[35]

So how do we overcome if we have been entangled by Satan's devices and have sinned in those areas? **By the word of our testimony (having walked in the light) and by the blood of the Lamb.**[36] God's word says that if someone will absolutely not admit his sin against you, to an individual, or even with two or three witnesses, then the whole church should be told.[37] The light saves us both individually and corporately, from the snares and traps that the enemy seeks to place in our lives.

The contrast:
Reasons why the enemy hates the light, hates people walking in the light, and will try to keep people in darkness –

1. **The light exposes the enemy as he is, and the destructive work he does**. He is a liar, murderer, destroyer and thief.[38] The light makes everything visible.[39] The light in our lives (Jesus in us) will show people up as they really are. The enemy hates being exposed.[40] The enemy (the devil) is the originator of every negative, destructive, vile thought, behaviour, or action. He wants you down in the slimy pit, to be trapped. Jesus wants us up with him, seated in heavenly realms.[41] Jesus wants you to exercise your **rightful** authority in this life over **all** the power of the enemy.

2. **The light will show the true nature of God**. We will have a right God-concept. He is merciful,[42] forgiving,[43] gracious,[44] kind,[45] loving,[46] generous,[47] and good.[48] We have quite a God! God's ways are higher than our ways.[49] Often people do not like God's ways, his mercy and grace, because all the glory and credit go to him. He always works for our good. He may discipline us to bring us to a better place with Jesus; to make us more loving, more forgiving, and more willing to walk in obedience to his ways. This is so we will bear much fruit. The Lord loves those he disciplines; he is treating us as sons.[50]

The devil hates God's people to believe and know how good, gracious and forgiving their God is: that Jesus is the way to heaven on earth, as well as our place in future glory. He will try to make people fear going to Jesus in times of need. Jesus would have us approach the *'throne of grace with confidence'* (Hebrews 4:16), because of the blood of Jesus, and the finished work of the cross. The devil's aim is to deceive God's people into believing they are not good enough, that they need to earn God's favour, or that God is not good, and that his ways are not good. Anything to prevent us going to our heavenly Father, to God, to have our needs met.[51]

His aim is to cause God's people to blame God for the harm the enemy has actually caused, and to rebel against him. He will always try to deceive people about God's nature. We need to rise above our natural thinking,[52] concerning events and circumstances, and stand **on the truth of God's word**. Blaming God will rob you of your joy, preventing you receiving from God, and living in your inheritance.

3.   The enemy wants us to be blind; blind to the truth of God's word, the truth of who Jesus is, and to the truth about other people! The Lord wants us to discern between good and evil, what is good and of him, and what is of the enemy.

Jesus wants us to stand against the devil's schemes and having put on the full armour of God, to **stand**,[53] and not follow other people into error.

4.   The enemy wants to deprive God's people of anything good in any way that he can. His only weapon is deception so that we believe lies about God, and God's people. We are to walk in the light. He does not want God's people to bear fruit and to shine, reflecting God's glory, because they have let the light of Jesus in.[54] Light is attractive and life-giving (without light there would be no life). People are drawn to the light, unless their deeds are evil. God's ability to forgive is more than a match for our evil deeds. Jesus overcame evil with good.[55] We are also to overcome evil with good, darkness with light.[56]

5.   The enemy hates the truth. He does not want people to know the truth. The light brings people into the truth. The entrance of God's word brings light.[57] Jesus said: '*I am the way and the truth and the life*' (John 14:6). The truth sets people free.[58] A truthful witness saves lives.[59] Jesus always wants people to be saved.[60]

God's people, those who belong to Jesus, listen to the truth. '*He who belongs to God hears what God says*' (John 8:47). God's word is the truth. We have the Spirit of truth in us.[61]

The reason that some people do not listen to the truth is because they do not belong to God.[62] Jesus said, '*Yet because I tell you the truth, you do not believe me'* (John 8:45). Lying is the devil's native language.[63] Jesus made very clear, that those who do not listen to him, are children of the devil, who is the father of lies. As God's people we **have** the Spirit of truth.[64]

6. **The enemy does not want you to know that scripture really works.** The enemy's aim is to keep us in darkness so we have no revelation of even where we are in bondage, no insight as to what the underlying problem is! As a result we seem to get continually 'tripped up' and defeated. The more we live in defeat, the less willing we are to get up, and try to walk closely with the Lord. I believe the light will reveal the area of difficulty, the underlying problem, and change this negative pattern, by the Holy Spirit: changing the feelings of resignation. Our defeated walk will become a victorious one.

The light and truth of God's word will expose where and when we are in error, when our lives are not based on the rock Jesus, and his word. We often get defeated because we depend either upon ourselves, and our natural giftings, or on others, instead of putting our trust and hope in Jesus. We also often put other people or things, before God. God says seek his Kingdom **first** and all these things will be added![65]

7. **Darkness hides.** It hides beauty as well as ugliness (sin and evil). The enemy does not want us to experience the joy of walking in the light. The enemy can easily deceive us when we walk in darkness. In these circumstances, Jesus needs the Body of Christ to be discerning. **Our** light will reveal their darkness. He tells us: *'to be wise as serpents and as innocent as doves'* (Matthew 10:16). We can choose to wilfully walk in the dark.

References

1. John 1:4–5
2. John 3:21
3. Ephesians 2:5, 8–9; 1 Corinthians 1:30
4. Romans 3:24; 4:1–5, 7; 6:23
5. 1 Corinthians 1:30; 2 Corinthians 5:21; Romans 3:22; 10:4
6. James 3:15–17; 1 Corinthians 1:31
7. Acts 26:18
8. 2 Corinthians 3:18
9. 1 Corinthians 10:13; Hebrews 2:18; 4:15

10. Ephesians 4:15–16; 1 Thessalonians 5:11
11. Luke 6:46; Matthew 7:24–25
12. John 8:45–47; 14:6; Titus 1:2
13. Mark 9:23–24; Luke 17:3–5; 1 Peter 1:7
14. Hebrews 4:15–16; Philippians 4:19
15. Psalm 51:6
16. 1 John 1:7–9
17. Matthew 3:6, 8; John 1:9
18. Matthew 23:26–28
19. 1 John 1:7; 2:10
20. 1 John 2:4–5, 10
21. 1 John 4:10–11; Hebrews 4:16; Philippians 4:13
22. Matthew 18:15–17; Galatians 6:1
23. 1 Corinthians 5:11; 6:9–10; Galatians 5:19–21
24. Matthew 9:6; 1 Corinthians 6:11; 15:3; Ephesians 2:1–6
25. Hebrews 7:25
26. 1 Peter 5:8–9; John 10:10
27. Romans 6:23
28. 1 Corinthians 5:9–11
29. 1 Corinthians 5:5
30. 1 Corinthians 5:13
31. 1 Corinthians 5:6
32. 1 Peter 2:9–11
33. 1 Corinthians 5:9–11; 6:9–11; Ephesians 2:1–4; Galatians 5:24; 2 Peter 2:20
34. 1 John 3:4–10; 2 Timothy 2:19
35. Galatians 5:16–25; Romans 8:1–14
36. Revelation 12:11
37. Matthew 18:15–17; 1 Timothy 5:19–20
38. John 8:44; 10:10
39. Ephesians 5:12–14
40. John 3:20
41. Ephesians 1:20–21; 2:6–7
42. Matthew 18:21–22
43. Ephesians 1:7–8
44. Ephesians 2:4–7
45. Matthew 14:16; 15:27–28
46. Psalm 25:10; 145:17; John 3:16
47. Matthew 20:1–16
48. Romans 8:28; Genesis 50:20
49. Isaiah 55:8–9
50. Hebrews 12:6
51. Philippians 4:19; Hebrews 4:16
52. Proverbs 3:5–6
53. Ephesians 6:11–18
54. John 3:21
55. Romans 5:8; Colossians 2:13–15
56. Romans 12:21; 1 Peter 3:9; Proverbs 25:21–22
57. Psalm 119:105, 130
58. John 8:31–32

59. Proverbs 14:25
60. John 3:16–17; 6:40
61. John 14:16–17; 16:13; 17:17
62. John 8:43–44
63. John 8:44
64. John 14:17; 15:26; 16:13
65. Matthew 6:33

Chapter 5

Walking in the Light Leads to Healthy, Loving Relationships

The greatest human need is to love and be loved. The world needs Jesus' love; no other 'love' will do. There are hearts aching to be loved and to have someone to love. Jesus can teach us to love. To love is to obey God's commands, then his love will be made complete in us.[1] This is very different from worldly love. *'Whoever has my commands and obeys them, he is the one who loves me. He who loves me will be loved by my Father, and I too will love him and show myself to him'* (John 14:21).[2] Walking in the light is obeying God's commands.[3] We can love because Jesus first loved us.[4] He showed us and continues to show us the way.

Jesus continually exhorts us to love one another. God is love. This love, Jesus' love is the only love that can satisfy the deepest human need. It is a love that is willing to lay down his or her life. When you are walking in obedience by faith, you are walking in love.

In the short-term, walking in the light may cause pain, but I believe that it will result in much fruit and joy that the world cannot take away.[5] Walking in darkness means hating our brothers. Strong words.[6] When you walk in darkness, you are not known. When we try to hide something or when we lie, this is darkness. We cause so much pain, mistrust and feelings of rejection. Lying is sin, and the wages of sin is death. Darkness and deceit remove the foundation for any good, trusting, lasting relationship. There is a false foundation, nothing to build upon. Light and darkness have no fellowship. There is no fellowship, no open dynamic relationship with light and darkness. There can be no fellowship with a person in wilful darkness (wilfully hiding, deceiving or lying) and a person in the light.[7]

The person who is hiding is either not trusting you, which is hurtful, or they do not want to be known by you. They are choosing to be in the dark. The area of any relationship in the dark affects other areas of that relationship. I believe that unless that person chooses to again walk in the light, that relationship will come to an 'end': it is static. When a person again chooses at any point to walk in the light; chooses Jesus, the relationship can then start to grow again and be built upon. It will be again a living, dynamic relationship, bearing fruit.

It is very costly to risk walking in the light again, especially if an area in the relationship has been wilfully hidden. This will reflect the value the person puts on the relationship, **and the person** they are in relationship with. He or she is valuing the relationship enough (and has a right fear of God),[8] to risk being rejected (by man). Rejection will happen unless the person is willing to forgive.

A person may initially feel unable or unwilling to forgive and accept us on discovering a difficult truth. If you value the relationship you will need to ask the Lord for his grace and strength to forgive them, giving them time to work through their emotions and feelings. You will need to put your security in Jesus. He is your rock. As you have been obedient to his word, walking in the light, the blood of Jesus still **cleanses you,**[9] even if the offended party does not forgive you! This will still cause pain. We can overcome in Jesus' strength.

On the other hand, if that person will forgive and accept, this will lead to a deeper, more secure loving relationship founded on God's word, walking in obedience with him. Jesus will be in that relationship, central in that area. The forgiven person will experience God's unconditional love. This will give courage to the person who has risked walking in the light, to continue to do so. It will also give to the forgiving person, the confidence that they will receive the same mercy and forgiveness as they walk in the light. It will be a faith-building step.

This is victory – two or more people walking in the light, praising God for the forgiveness and cleansing of Jesus, knowing: *'There is now no condemnation for those who are in Christ Jesus'* (Romans 8:1). They will be in fellowship. A genuine trust will be built, fruit borne. There will be the beginnings of a right foundation, as you continue to walk in the truth and light. The relationship will become more real and satisfying, problems will be faced and tackled, solutions discovered in the light of God's word.

It is not easy to walk in the light and face issues, sometimes long buried. We need encouragement. Jesus will walk through every step with us! We need to be like Jesus to others, to continually encourage them to love and forgive.

Some people may say 'you do not need to confess your sins to one another. You just need to confess them to the Lord. He can forgive you.' Indeed he can. It is good to communicate with Jesus about **all** areas of our lives, to be in a loving relationship with him. In scripture it also says confess your sins to another, so we can be forgiven **and** healed.[10] To be healed we need to pray. It also says **whatever you** forgive, will be forgiven, and whatever you do not forgive, will not be forgiven.[11] Jesus has given us authority to forgive.[12] We need to walk in the light and exercise our authority for good. We need each other in this area.

This is such a challenge for us, God's people, and such a rare walk. We have a high calling. I believe we will not be the people God has called us to **be** or ever reach our God-given potential, our God-given goals, unless we meet the challenge of walking in the light as Jesus walked.[13]

Walking in the light gets our lives built on rock,[14] a right foundation on reality, on Jesus. This foundation, I believe, is needed for a deeper, lasting work of healing and deliverance to happen in our lives.

Walking in the light does not demand perfection. You need no degrees or diplomas. You do not need to be of a certain culture, race or creed. You just need to accept Jesus as Lord, be willing to follow him and obey him. He will satisfy your deepest needs. Grasping and taking will never meet your need; God's hand is against that.

I pray that by God's grace and in his strength, you will begin to know the joy and freedom of walking in the light of his presence, getting the **victory** over the enemy's lying tactics, aiming to pull you down as you choose to submit to God's word and his ways. *'All the ways of the Lord are loving and faithful for those who keep the demands of his covenant'* (Psalm 25:10).

References

1. 1 John 2:5; 4:12, 16–18
2. John 14:21; 15:9–10; 1 John 4:10–12
3. 1 John 1:5–7
4. 1 John 4:9–12
5. John 15:10–12; 16:22–24
6. 1 John 2:10–11
7. 2 Corinthians 6:14; Ephesians 5:11
8. Proverbs 2:1–5; 3:7
9. 1 John 1:7–9
10. James 5:16
11. John 20:23
12. 2 Corinthians 2:10–11; Colossians 3:13; Ephesians 4:32
13. John 1:4–5, 9; 3:19; 8:12; 1 John 1:5–6; 2:6
14. Matthew 7:24–25

PART 2

Letting Our Light Shine

'You are the light of the world.'

(Matthew 5:14)

Chapter 6

Reasons We Find Difficulty in Letting Our Light Shine

There are many negative aspects of our lives which need to be brought into the light, dealt with and forgiven. This is a process which may take many years; you may have been the dumping ground for all sorts of negative behaviour from parents and others in authority.

Once we have dealt with the negative (there may be issues that God brings into the light further on in our walk with him), we can now **start** to walk in the **victory**, the grace and the abundance of the positive. This is the truth of who we are, what Jesus has done and the gifts and talents he has given us.[1] We are the light of the world. *'You are the light of the world'* (Matthew 5:14). *'Let your light shine before men that they may see your good deeds and praise your Father in heaven'* (Matthew 5:16). This can be difficult. We must avoid getting stuck in the negative but we are to overcome and walk in the *'good works which God prepared in advance for us'* (Ephesians 2:10).

There are many reasons why we may find difficulty in letting our light shine

1. **We are ashamed** we belong to Jesus. Jesus says *'whoever acknowledges me before men, I will also acknowledge him before my Father in heaven. But whoever disowns me before men, I will disown'* (Matthew 10:32–33). We need to know who we are in Jesus, and what an incredible honour and privilege it is to be a

co-heir with him, and to be seated with him in heavenly realms. We need to understand exactly what he has done for us. Do you know anyone else who would stoop down for you? *'You stoop down to make me great'* (Psalm 18:35). He walked with us. He chose to die for us so we can be forgiven and have access to God, to be with him in glory. Do you know anyone else who accepts you,[2] forgives you,[3] and would die for you?

If we are **for** Jesus, he will never put us to shame.[4] The world needs to know it is God's people who have been blessed.

2. **We fear other people's opinions of us**; their judgements and criticisms. We need to be secure in the knowledge of God's love for us, his affirmation of us, as we walk according to his will in the light.

3. **We feel condemned**. We feel we fall so short of his call, and his glory. This happens because we have not walked in the light, allowing the blood of Jesus to cleanse us from all the resentment, the bitterness, the hatred. We have just suppressed all these negative emotions. As a result, we feel we cannot speak in accordance with the truth, because

(a) we don't live up to what we confess, or

(b) we don't believe in our hearts the truth.

We need to know it is by grace we are saved. We cannot earn our salvation. *'For it is by grace you have been saved, through faith – and this is not from yourselves, it is the gift of God – not by works, so that no-one can boast'* (Ephesians 2:8). *'Let him who boasts boast in the Lord'* (1 Corinthians 1:31).

4. **False humility**. This is a destructive and paralysing attitude. The feeling of 'I don't want them to feel bad, because I've got so much, and they've got so little' – so we underachieve, belittle ourselves to fit in, to be accepted. We may even try to hide our gifts and talents. There is the fear of being rejected when we excel. The fear of being rejected because we have so much, and we reflect Jesus and his love. We try to avoid being in conflict with other, people's jealousies and selfish ambition. We are not to let other people's inadequacies and shortcomings 'squash' us into a mould, preventing our gifts and talents being used. *'Do not conform any longer to the*

pattern of this world, but be transformed by the renewing of your mind' (Romans 12:2).

*'The Lord will be **your** confidence'* (Proverbs 3:26). The enemy will constantly try to prevent you from expressing and developing your God-given gifts, talents, and the person he created you to be. We need to be able to acknowledge that it is God who is the giver.[5] It is God who had made us fearfully and wonderfully in his image.[6] We are God's workmanship.[7] We are to live for the praise of him who made us. We need to know that it is God who has chosen us, each of us is unique. *'Do not be afraid, little flock, for your Father has been pleased to give you the Kingdom'* (Luke 12:32).

5. **Fear of failure**. We fear the expectations put on us. We are fearful that people knowing our gifts, talents and our ability, will put expectations upon us. People will see our 'failure' as well as the achievements and successes. We may feel it is easier to hide, our gifts and talents, rather than be seen to 'fail'.

We are to overcome that fear of 'failure'. The saying that 'success is failure turned inside out' has an element of sense. If you have ever 'failed', that is when the Lord teaches us, it is not an end. We are to learn from our mistakes; when we fall short of our goal. His love is not dependent on our achievements.

We learn to put our faith, hope and trust in him, not in our abilities. I believe real or perceived 'failure' is often a door for greater fruitfulness, as we learn to persevere, overcome and discover the reason why we didn't achieve the goal of success intended.

We need to know that underneath are God's everlasting arms. If the activity is of God, and God's desire is for you to succeed[8] in a given area (and I believe it is God's desire for us to succeed and give him the glory), he will continue to teach us and act on our behalf, until we achieve our desired goal.

God is faithful. He will do it. *'Anyone who trusts in him will never be put to shame'* (Romans 10:11).

6. **Fear of risk**. When we learn new skills or apply our gifts and talents to a new venture, there is always an element of

risk. We may fear we will not achieve our goal or that we may lose personally, financially or in some other way. Do not entertain such thoughts. Jesus is our rock. We are to include Jesus. He always knows the way[9] for us to go forward. He is able to lead us through all the difficulties. We walk by faith. We are to put our hand in his. We are to be courageous.

If we are fighting for justice for someone, or some dream, goal, or given situation where our personal gifts and talents are involved, there is a risk. God loves faith and faithfulness. He loves his people to step forward in faith, in response to him. We need to put our faith and our hope in God's word for us. It is his word that will not fail. **He will not fail or forsake us**. *'Never will I leave you; never will I forsake you'* (Hebrews 13:5). God always fulfils his promises to us. *'For no matter how many promises God has made, they are "Yes" in Christ.'*[10] *'With God all things are possible'* (Matthew 19:26).

7. **Fear of persecution**. Persecution[11] is reality; it happens. *'In fact, everyone who wants to live a godly life in Christ Jesus will be persecuted'* (2 Timothy 3:12). The enemy doesn't mind so much if our gifts are hidden, or we hide the truth. We will be opposed as we walk in the light and the truth.

We need to overcome that fear of persecution, sown by the enemy. I believe persecution is for a season and a reason. God is always working. We need to have a right knowledge of **who** is in control, and **who** exactly can harm us. God is in control, the enemy cannot touch us (as we walk in obedience, submitted to his word) apart from God's will, plan and purpose. *'Though they plot evil against you and devise wicked schemes, they cannot succeed'* (Psalm 21:11). *'Do not be afraid of those who kill the body but cannot kill the soul. Rather, be afraid of the one who can destroy both soul and body in hell'* (Matthew 10:28). The devil can kill the body but not us. We have been given two promises: firstly, the gift of eternal life,[12] and secondly, that no-one can snatch us from God's, or Jesus', hand.[13] *'Do not fear what they fear; do not be frightened. But in your hearts set apart Christ as Lord'* (1 Peter 3:14–15). Fear of man is a snare. **Nothing can touch us apart from the knowledge and will of God.**[14] *'Are not two sparrows sold for* *a penny? Yet not one of them will fall to the ground apart from the will of your Father'* (Matthew 10:29–30). No-one could touch or harm the Lord Jesus until the set time. *'This man was handed over to you by God's set purpose and foreknowledge'* (Acts 2:23). God is in control. Even death could not hold him. *'It was impossible for death to keep its hold on him'* (Acts 2:24).

We will be opposed for belonging to Jesus, for acknowledging his Lordship. Some people do not want good, the light and righteousness to win. Wicked [15] people and those who have not dealt with their sinful nature. Some people will not want to rejoice with us when we succeed, when we have used our gifts and talents for the extension of the Kingdom and for God's glory.

Nothing can separate us from God's love.[16] Nor can anything prevent us being raised up.[17] Don't allow the enemy's sown fear of persecution stop you doing good and using all your gifts, talents and strengths for God's Kingdom. The right fear of the Lord is the beginning of wisdom. People will see, as we walk in the light, the way in which we respond to being persecuted. We are not to be afraid in any way. This is a sign we will be saved.[18]

How does the enemy try to prevent us walking in the light – in the good works God has for us?

1. **Intimidation**: by trying to make us believe they are stronger than us, or have some power over us, or that they have power to harm us. They have not. Jesus is Lord. We are seated with him in heavenly places. The enemy is under our feet. They will try to make us stop doing good. They say, or imply, if you carry on speaking for Jesus, and acting in his name, you will be harmed. The disciples were threatened: *'After further threats they let them go'* (Acts 4:21). The disciples knew their authority. They were not deterred. We need to know ours, that we have been given authority over the enemy.[19] They went to the Lord in prayer. *'Now, Lord, consider their threats and enable your servants to speak your word with great boldness. Stretch out your hand to heal'* (Acts 4:29–30).

Our enemies cannot stop God's plan or purpose succeeding.

'If their purpose or activity is of human origin, it will fail. But if it is from God, you will not be able to stop these men' (Acts 5:38–39). *'There is no wisdom, no insight, no plan that can succeed against the Lord'* (Proverbs 21:30).

  2. **Opposition**: people will try to put obstacles in your path. They may try to physically hurt or abuse you, to try to prevent you using your gifts and talents for God's glory. They might try to take what is rightfully yours, to use what God has given you for ungodly goals. They will fail.[20] We are to continue, to persevere:

- *'If God is **for us**, who can be against us? He who did not spare his own Son, but gave him up for us all – how will he not also, along with him, graciously give us all things?'* (Romans 8:32).

- If we are obedient to God, and his ways, doing what he says, he will be an enemy unto our enemies, and he will oppose those who oppose us (Exodus 23:22). He will fight for us.

- We are to commit ourselves to our faithful Creator and continue to do good. *'So then, those who suffer according to God's will, should commit themselves to their faithful Creator, and continue to do good'* (1 Peter 4:19).

- We are *'to imitate those who through faith and patience inherit what has been promised'* (Hebrews 6:12).

Again, *'There is no wisdom, no insight, no plan, that can succeed against the Lord'* (Proverbs 21:30). We are called to be overcomers.[21]

  3. **Rejection**: people will try to prevent you doing God's will by:

(a) **rejecting the person you are**. We need to know our value and acceptance in Jesus. We need to know that it was Jesus, although rejected by men, who had the full acceptance of his heavenly Father because of his love for him and his submission to his will (not the enemy's or the world's will). *'The stone you builders rejected has become the capstone'* (Acts 4:11; Psalm 118:22). What men accept is not necessarily what God accepts. His ways are higher and different from ours (Isaiah 55:8–9). God chose the foolish things of the world to shame the wise.[22] God gives his kingdom to those who produce its fruit.[23]

(b) **rejecting what we are doing**, what we are trying to achieve. If what you are doing is of God, they will not be able to destroy your work. *'You did not choose me, but I chose you and appointed you to go and bear fruit – **fruit that will last**'* (John 15:16). God is able to keep what has been entrusted to him.[24] God is our refuge, our ever-present help.

4. Shut doors: the enemy will try to shut doors that are meant to be open – to prevent us doing good. Jesus opens and shuts doors. *'What he opens **no-one** can shut, and what he shuts **no-one** can open. I know your deeds. See, **I have** placed before you an open door that no-one can shut'* (Revelation 3:7–8). Jesus is the door, the gate.[25]

God is able. Peter was in jail, but an angel of the Lord guided him through the jail into freedom. *'They passed the first and second guards and came to the iron gate leading to the city. It opened **for** them by itself, and they went through it'* (Acts 12:10) [26] *'But Peter kept on knocking, and when they opened the door and saw him, they were astonished'* (Acts 12:16). *'Knock and the door will be opened to you'* (Matthew 7:7).[27] Jesus is the one who shuts and opens doors. We need to be in that place of obedience to Jesus where, when we walk towards a door it automatically opens. *'This is what the Lord says to his anointed ... to open doors before him, so that gates will not be shut'* (Isaiah 45:1). Neither can the enemy trap you into limiting situations.

5. Ridicule: people may mock and make fun of our values and standards, with such comments as 'You're silly, that's a silly idea – that's impossible; you're just a dreamer, be practical.' Human reasoning is an enemy of God's work, which is by faith. We put our trust in him and his word for us.

We are not to listen to those lies that try to cause us to doubt what we are doing, and our faith. God will act on our behalf and show them who is in control. If we persevere doing good he will show them who is in control and prove to them the wisdom of God. *'Where is the wise man? Where is the* scholar? Where is the philosopher of this age? Has not God made foolish the wisdom of the world? For since in the wisdom of God the world through its wisdom did not know him' (1 Corinthians 1:20–21). We are to set our minds on things above where Christ is. *'Set your minds on things above, not on earthly things. For you died, and your life is now hidden with Christ in God'* (Colossians 3:2–3).

We are sons of God, led by God's Holy Spirit. *'Those who are led by the Spirit of God are sons of God. For you did not receive a spirit that makes you a slave again to fear, but you received a Spirit of Sonship'* (Romans 8:14–15).

6. **Discouragement**. All the work of the enemy is discouragement, ridicule, rejection, and opposition. The enemy will try to discourage us when we see wicked men apparently prospering. God says, *'Do not fret because of evil men or be envious of those who do wrong; for like the grass they will soon wither'* (Psalm 37:1–2). *'A little while, and the wicked will be no more'* (Psalm 37:10).[28] The Lord will vindicate those who trust and look up to him. *'You will again see the distinction between the righteous and the wicked, between those who serve God and those who do not'* (Malachi 3:18). The Lord loves the just and will not forsake his faithful ones.[29] *'Do not throw away your confidence, it will be richly rewarded. You need to persevere so that, when you have done the will of God, you will receive what he has promised'* (Hebrews 10:35). He will exalt us. We are the people who will inherit the land. We will triumph. We will look upon our enemies in triumph.[30]

7. **The enemy will try to cause us to sin**. The enemy will try to tempt us and entice us to do wrong. We can never beat our enemies by retaliation, or we become an enemy ourselves.

8. **Fear of comparison**. We have all been given different gifts and talents, a unique blend and combination for a unique purpose. We are people on whom God has chosen to lavish his love,[31] and to pour out on us, gifts and talents.[32] We are made in the image of God,[33] and have intrinsic value and worth, not dependent on our gifts. God does not put more or less value on a person dependent on their gifts.

Our confidence and boasting is in God. *'The Lord will be your confidence'* (Proverbs 3:26). *'Every good and perfect gift is from above'* (James 1:17).[34] We are to use all our gifts and talents. We all have **different** gifts and talents. We are not to put more value on others' gifts above our own. That only leads to jealousy, and envy. We are not to live in comparison with others, but reach our own potential.

References

1. 1 Corinthians 12:27–31; Romans 12:4–7; Ephesians 4:7, 11–13
2. Ephesians 1:4–5; Psalm 27:10; John 6:37
3. 1 Corinthians 15:3; 1 John 1:9
4. Romans 10:11
5. James 1:17
6. Psalm 139:14
7. Ephesians 2:10
8. Deuteronomy 28:13
9. Isaiah 43:1–3; 48:17; John 14:6
10. Joshua 23:14; 2 Corinthians 1:20
11. Matthew 13:21; John 15:20
12. Romans 6:23
13. John 10:28–29
14. Matthew 10:29
15. 2 Thessalonians 3:2–3
16. Romans 8:38–39
17. John 6:39–40
18. Philippians 1:27–30
19. Luke 10:18–20
20. Psalm 21:11
21. 1 John 5:4–5
22. 1 Corinthians 1:27
23. Matthew 21:43
24. 2 Timothy 1:12
25. John 10:7, 9
26. Acts 5:19
27. Isaiah 45:1–2
28. Psalm 37:20
29. Psalm 97:10
30. Psalm 118:6–7
31. 1 John 3:1
32. Ephesians 4:6–11; Matthew 25:14–15
33. Genesis 1:26
34. Ephesians 4:8

Chapter 7

Who We Are,
and the Character We Reflect

Jesus is the light of the world,[1] that light is the life of men. *'In him was life, and that life was the light of men'* (John 1:4). People will see Jesus in us. *'Christ in you, the hope of glory'* (Colossians 1:27). As we commit our way to the Lord *'he will make your righteousness shine like the dawn, the justice of your cause like the noon day'* (Psalm 37:6). *'The path of the righteous is like the first gleam of dawn, shining ever brighter till the full light of day'* (Proverbs 4:18).

We are led by God's Holy Spirit. We reflect God's nature when we become believers (we are **born** of God). We continue to reflect his nature more and more[2] as we walk in obedience, and allow him into more areas of our lives to change, heal and forgive. We are, and will become, a people totally different from the world.[3] We are to live as children of the light.[4] The light will show who we are. We are ambassadors for Christ on this earth. We will reflect his victory and his ability to overcome. *'But thanks be to God, who always leads us in triumphal procession in Christ, and through **us** spreads everywhere the fragrance of the knowledge of him'* (2 Corinthians 2:14).

We have a deposit of God's Holy Spirit within us as a seal of ownership guaranteeing what is to come. God's love has been poured out into our hearts. *'And hope does not disappoint us, because God has poured out his love into our hearts by the Holy*

Spirit, whom he has given us' (Romans 5:5). Christ's nature in us affects our behaviour, attitudes, and values.

People of the world live only to gratify their sinful nature and their earthly desires (Ephesians 2:1–3).

(a) They are in darkness (Ephesians 5:8).

(b) They are condemned, they are still in their sins, they are under God's wrath (Ephesians 2:3). They are not forgiven and to receive salvation, I believe they personally need to accept Jesus, his forgiveness, and to believe on his name.

(c) Outside Christ people are involved in fruitless deeds of darkness (Ephesians 5:11).

(d) People outside of Jesus are 'alienated from God', and are his enemies because of their evil behaviour (Colossians 1:21).

(e) They are dead in their sin. *'The wages of sin is death but the gift of God is eternal life in Christ Jesus our Lord' (Romans 6:23).*

(f) They are without hope and without God in the world (Ephesians 2:12). They are cut off from their source of potential, their Creator God, because of their sin causing them to be the enemies of God and creating a wall of hostility. The light will expose them and what they do. The light will also show them the way to Jesus, if they choose.

By our character and nature

There is a depth to our lives as we have gone through trials [5] and tribulations.[6] We rejoice in our sufferings because we know suffering produces perseverance, character, and hope. And hope does not disappoint us because *'God has poured out his love into our hearts by the Holy Spirit'* (Romans 5:5).

The fruit of God's Holy Spirit in our lives has an effect on our character and natures. *'But the fruit of the Spirit is love, joy, peace, patience, kindness, goodness, faithfulness, gentleness, and self-control. Against such things there is no law. Those who belong to Christ Jesus have crucified the sinful nature with its passion and desires'* (Galatians 5:22–25).

1.   We have a **love** which springs from the knowledge of God's love for us, and his forgiveness of us. Every good work springs from our love and faith.[7] To know what real love is, unconditional love, we need to know our God. So often the 'love' people know in the world is conditional. People using and taking rather than giving freely. We can freely give because God freely gave to and loves us[8] when we accepted and believed in him. We love because God has poured his love into our hearts.[9] We love because he first loved us.[10]

Our love is forgiving and giving. Our new nature is loving. **We know** that those who are in obedience to the Lord are loving. We will receive and know God's love through his people, who are in obedience. People who love do not accept compromise (on God's word), give in to wrong, or accept just some of the truth. **We have the ability to love with all our heart.**[11]

2.   We have **joy**. We have a joy, an inner joy that the world and persecution cannot take away (John 16:22–24).[12] Our enemies will try to make us downcast, melancholy, despondent, even depressed. We can overcome and be victorious in this area and **be seen to be so**. Our joy springs from an inner knowledge of:

(a)   Jesus who will never leave, forsake or fail us;
(b)   the hope, Jesus is coming again to receive his own;[13]
(c)   the hope of salvation, salvation of our souls;[14]
(d)   the hope of our future reward (despite our present trials). The hope of our inheritance that can never perish, spoil or fade;[15]
(e)   the hope and the knowledge that our enemies will be defeated and that Jesus has triumphed.

These all give us a hope and an inner joy.

The knowledge that we are walking in the will of, and in obedience to God, gives us an inner joy. Depression is often caused by unforgiveness, hurt, and suppressed anger. We need to walk in the light, the fruit of which will be joy as the blood of Jesus cleanses us from all sin, and the darkness is replaced with the light of Jesus. We then have the joy of being forgiven and accepted **not** condemned. The **joy** of the Lord is our strength.

3. We have **peace**. God gives us a peace.[16] A peace the world neither knows nor understands. The enemy tries to stir up confusion and anxiety. The knowledge of God's will and being in his will gives us peace. The knowledge of his control. We have a peace beyond understanding when our security is in God – his ability, his enabling, his protection and his love for us. His ability to keep and save. The knowledge that Jesus is Lord and in control despite circumstances to the contrary, protects our hearts and minds.

When the enemy does stir up turmoil, anxiety and related fear, we need to pray,[17] getting into the Lord's presence (with another believer, if possible), and confess our feelings to God. By his Holy Spirit, he will give us a better **godly** perspective on the situation, giving us peace. *'Let the peace of Christ rule in your hearts, since as members of one body you were called to peace'* (Colossians 3:15).

There is also a peace as opposed to conflict (fighting and animosity). Jesus destroyed the dividing wall of hostility between believers (people who have accepted his forgiveness and himself), because of the work on the cross. *'Peacemakers who sow in peace raise a harvest of righteousness'* (James 3:18). We are different from the world.

4. We have **patience**. We learn to endure. *'So do not throw away your confidence; it will be richly rewarded. You need to persevere so that when you have done the will of God, you will receive what he has promised'* (Hebrews 10:35).

The fruit of our lives is patience when faced with suffering, knowing:

(a) God's faithfulness;

(b) his hand is at work;

(c) he will reward us as we remain faithful;

(d) our enemies, those who persecute and trouble us, will be defeated.[18] We are not to rebel and go into sin. *'We consider blessed those who have persevered. You have heard of Job's perseverance and have seen what the Lord finally brought about'* (James 5:10–11). Love **never** gives up;[19]

(e) other people are going through the same trials as our-
     selves.[20] We can stand together.

We need to learn to persevere, to overcome obstacles and
have patience to **wait** for God to act on our behalf! We need
to be people who are relentless. We will get the victory and
overcome the powers of darkness as we relentlessly persevere
and hold onto the **truth**. We reflect something of the love and
character of Jesus when we are patient, with others, with
ourselves, or with our circumstances.

5. We are **kind**. There is a kindness in our nature, we
ourselves having received God's mercy in his acceptance and
forgiveness of us. God has been kind to us, *'And God raised us
up with Christ and seated us with him in the heavenly realms in
Christ Jesus, in order that in the coming ages he might show the
incomparable riches of his grace, expressed **in his kindness** to us in
Christ Jesus'* (Ephesians 2:6–7). He didn't write us off when we
sinned nor did he rub our noses in the wrong we had done.
He freely forgave us in the one he loved, Jesus.[21]

Malice, spitefulness, negative words, can easily wound,
but

(a) kindness and kind words heal and soothe. They affirm
     and lift **up**;

(b) kindness covers sin and doesn't 'repeat' a matter, doesn't
     keep bringing up a wrong which has been confessed and
     repented of. *'He who covers over an offence promotes love,
     but whoever repeats the matter separates close friends'*
     (Proverbs 17:9);

(c) kindness can be expressed in deeds. We are to be kind in
     deed also, and affirm a person who is feeling hurt,
     betrayed or who has fallen short, or perceived themselves
     to have done so. *'He who is kind to the poor lends to the
     Lord, and he will reward him for what he has done'* (Proverbs
     19:17).

We will also gain the respect of outsiders,[22] letting our light
shine.

6. **Goodness**. *'Even a child is known by his actions, by
whether his conduct is pure and righteous'* (Proverbs 20:11). *'Good
deeds are obvious, and even those that are not cannot be hidden'*

(1 Timothy 5:25). There is a good heart-motive in a good person, whose goal is to help the poor, the oppressed, and those in need, and **to endeavour to secure justice for those who have been wrongly treated**, misled, or abused. We are not doing good for gain. Who we are determines what we do. *'Likewise every **good tree bears good fruit**, but a bad tree bears bad fruit. A good tree cannot bear bad fruit, ... but a bad tree cannot bear good fruit'* (Matthew 7:17–18). Goodness will be acknowledged, even publicly.[23]

'Evil men will bow down in the presence of the good, and the wicked at the gates of the righteous' (Proverbs 14:19). God has stored up goodness for us. God will publicly show his goodness towards us.[24]

7. **Faithfulness**. This is so valuable. An ability to stand firm, remain faithful to:

(a) what we **believe** – the truth of God's word; who Jesus is, and what he has done;

(b) what **we are called to do**; and

(c) **the people we are in relationship with**, despite the turmoil, the trials, the persecution, the opposition, and the temptations, of the world. We remain faithful. *'Many a man claims to have unfailing love, **but a faithful man who can find?**'* (Proverbs 20:6).

This kind of faithfulness is born in our lives as we learn of God's faithfulness towards us. His complete dependability. His absolute truthfulness, his ability to forgive, and his motive for our good. We know his promises towards us are sure and can be trusted, as are his warnings, which are to be feared. Faithfulness walks hand in hand with love. A faithful person is someone who does not let us down, pretend to be something, when they are not at all like they portray themselves to be. A person who both puts his hope and faith **first in God**. And from that secure place, in the knowledge of God's love for them, they remain faithful to us. God is faithful. He will do it.[25] We should be known for our faithfulness.

8. **Gentleness** – as opposed to abrasiveness and harshness. *'A gentle answer turns away wrath, but a harsh word stirs up anger'* (Proverbs 15:1). Our gentleness will help people to

respond to us and to the message of the gospel. Our gentleness understands man's frailty, his weakness, understands the need for us to be instructed, and guided in God's ways. When we are gentle, we are not overbearing or demanding. This only causes people to be stiff-necked, and resistant; unresponsive and unyielding to what we say. Our gentleness should be evident.

9. **Self-control**. What an important fruit of God's Holy Spirit. To be able to control our tongue, control our anger, control our physical appetites, including our consumption of food, and sexual appetite. The need to channel our strengths and energy in right ways. A self-controlled person is a disciplined person, who has learned to channel his energy productively: learning to overcome sinful natures and sinful desires. The enemy's aim will always be to stir up ungodly emotions, causing us to act out of control, wrongly or impulsively, from anger, fear, and lust. The more we acknowledge the Lord's control and our dependence on him, the more we will be in control of our choices, desires and actions, and the less we will need to 'control' others in ungodly ways, by ungodly means. Our enemies will submit to us. We will not lose our temper or retaliate in trying circumstances. Our God is on the throne. Jesus is Lord. We will demonstrate a strength of character to the world.

How will these qualities help us overcome our enemies?

1. **They will help us to secure our eternal inheritance**, helping us to bear fruit, being productive. *'For this very reason, make every effort to add to your faith goodness; and to goodness, knowledge; and to knowledge, self-control; and to self-control, perseverance; and to perseverance, godliness; and to godliness, brotherly kindness; and to brotherly kindness, love. For if you possess these qualities in increasing measure, they will keep you from being ineffective and unproductive in your knowledge of our Lord'* (2 Peter 1:5–8). *'... and you will receive a rich welcome into the eternal kingdom of our Lord and Saviour, Jesus Christ'* (2 Peter 1:11).

2. **They will keep us from falling.**[26] *'For if you do these things, you will never fall'* (2 Peter 1:10). The enemy's aim is to keep us out of the Kingdom of God, and once in the Kingdom of God to try to keep us from receiving our inheritance as a reward. He wants us to fail, and to fall away from the living God. The enemy certainly doesn't want us bearing good fruit, for God's glory.

3. **Our good nature will help us in our daily walk.** Those who would want to stir up trouble for us and oppose us, will see our good behaviour and will not be able to accuse or slander us. Our goodness will be evident.[27]

4. **We will 'shine', leading others to salvation.** People will see our good behaviour and choose to believe in the name of Jesus and be saved. We will be a light for them. We have a merciful God. He chose to die for us even when we were his enemies.[28] He chose to forgive us. It is God's goodness and kindness that leads to repentance. We may help to lead others to Jesus by our goodness, and love.

Those who have been 'trapped into doing the devil's will'[29] will discern or recognize, because of the light, their error, and they too will return to their living Saviour. If a person repents and returns to Jesus, then an enemy has become a friend. If a person comes to a living relationship with Jesus (a saving knowledge of him), another enemy has become a friend. And, in him, they too can walk in the light and bear fruit for Jesus, and to begin themselves to overcome evil with good. Light shows the way. Our light shows the way. Jesus is the light. We will help to *'turn them* (unbelievers) *from darkness to light, and from the power of Satan to God, so that they may* **receive forgiveness of sins** *and a place among those who are sanctified by faith'* in Jesus (Acts 26:18). By our behaviour we love, give and forgive them, giving them every opportunity and desire to turn to Jesus. God is not willing that anyone should perish but repent and come to a saving knowledge of himself. But if people choose to continue to be our and God's enemy, it is God who will act on our behalf.

'It is mine to avenge; I will repay, says the Lord' (Romans 12:19), and *'No weapon forged against you will prevail'* (Isaiah

54:17). He will not allow our enemies to harm us or snatch us from his hand.[30]

5. We will shine, **we will be known to be the sons and daughters of the living God**. We will shine like stars. *'You shine like stars in the universe as you hold out the word of life'* (Philippians 2:15–16). We have the light of God shining in our hearts. *'We have this treasure in jars of clay to show that this all-surpassing power is from God and not from us'* (2 Corinthians 4:7). We are a different people, and will be seen to be a different people.

References

1. John 8:12
2. 2 Corinthians 3:18; Galatians 5:22–24; Philippians 1:6
3. 1 John 2:15–17; 1 Peter 2:9–10; James 4:4
4. Ephesians 5:8
5. 1 Peter 1:6; James 1:2–4
6. Acts 14:22; John 16:33
7. 1 Thessalonians 1:3; 2 Thessalonians 1:11
8. 1 Corinthians 2:12
9. Romans 5:5
10. 1 John 4:19
11. Romans 5:5; Matthew 22:37–39; Luke 10:27; Ephesians 6:7; Colossians 3:23
12. 2 Corinthians 7:4
13. 1 Thessalonians 4:17; Acts 1:11; Matthew 24:27; 2 Thessalonians 1:7
14. 1 Peter 1:7–9
15. 1 Peter 1:3–4
16. John 14:27; 16:33
17. Philippians 4:6–7
18. 2 Thessalonians 1:5–10
19. 1 Corinthians 13:8
20. Philippians 1:28–30
21. Matthew 10:8; Romans 3:24; 1 Corinthians 2:12; Ephesians 2:3–5
22. Proverbs 11:16–17
23. Psalm 23:5–6; 31:19
24. Psalm 23:5–6; 31:19
25. 1 Thessalonians 5:24
26. 2 Peter 1:5–8, 10; Psalm 15
27. 1 Peter 2:12
28. Romans 5:10
29. 2 Timothy 2:25–26
30. John 10:27–30; Romans 8:28, 37–39

Chapter 8

The Way in Which We Live

1. Our goals and ambitions

Our goals and ambitions will reflect who we are. *'Do nothing out of selfish ambition or vain conceit, but in humility consider others better than yourselves'* (Philippians 2:3). We are not to provoke and envy one another. Our goal is to please God.[1] We walk according to God's Spirit, in obedience. We live our lives according to God's word, in obedience. We have:

(a) the knowledge of God's ways, that he rewards;[2]
(b) the knowledge that God has a plan and purpose for our lives, in which we can walk.[3]

We are sons of God and are led by his Holy Spirit. We put to death the deeds of the sinful nature. The fruits of the Spirit-filled life, as we walk in obedience, are *'love, joy, peace, patience, kindness, goodness, faithfulness, gentleness and self-control'* (Galatians 5:22–23). *'He himself bore our sins in his body on the tree, so that we might die to sins, and **live** for righteousness'* (1 Peter 2:24).

The world gratifies the desires of the sinful nature, and they are often motivated by greed, envy, lust or malice. They are people who simply live for themselves in a finite existence. The light will enable others to see our goals and activities are different.

2. Our motives are different

Our good works spring from our faith. We do not do good to

seek approval, gain favour or to earn our salvation. We do need to be affirmed and encouraged by other believers. *'Spur one another on towards love and good deeds'* (Hebrews 10:24). We know we are *'God's workmanship, created in Christ Jesus to do good works, which God prepared in advance for us to do'* (Ephesians 2:10).

We live for God.[4] *'The world and its desires pass away, but the man who does the will of God lives for ever'* (1 John 2:17). I believe we have God-given goals, dreams, and desires to fulfil, ***'for it is God who works in you to will and to act according to his good purpose'*** (Philippians 2:13).

We have an eternal perspective. God is not willing that anyone should perish but that all men may come to a saving knowledge of himself.

3. Our dependence is different

Our dependence, our hope and our trust are in God and Jesus and his ability to save and keep. We are not to depend upon worldly wealth, fame, approval or to put our hope and dependence in other people. *'Some trust in chariots and some in horses, but we trust in the name of the Lord our God. They are brought to their knees and fall, but we rise up and stand firm'* (Psalm 20:7–8). *'A horse is vain hope for deliverance; despite its great strength it cannot save'* (Psalm 33:17–18). God is utterly dependable (Titus 1:2).

Our trust and faith and hope are in God to save, deliver, uphold, to supply all our needs. *'And my God will meet all your needs according to his glorious riches in Christ Jesus'* (Philippians 4:19). We are to go boldly to the throne of grace and to ask. We have a God in heaven. *'Let us then approach the throne of grace with confidence, so that we may receive mercy and find grace to help us in our time of need'* (Hebrews 4:16). Jesus promises, *'And I will do whatever you ask in my name, so that the Son may bring glory to the Father'* (John 14:13).

God's grace is sufficient for **us**. Our dependence is on God. From a place of security we are able to stand; we are able to give.

4. As God's people we walk by faith

What a different way to walk. *'Without faith it is impossible to please God'* (Hebrews 11:6). We enter into the saving work of the cross by faith in Jesus, believing and accepting him. Our lives should continue by faith, walking according to God's promises, in his word. We continue to walk by faith as we appropriate and believe God's word and God's promises for us. *'For no matter how many promises God has made, they are "Yes" in Christ. And so through him the "Amen" is spoken by us to the glory of God'* (2 Corinthians 1:20). Abraham believed God and it was credited to him as righteousness. *'The righteous will live by faith'* (Romans 1:17). We act because we believe. *'The life I live in the body, I live by faith in the Son of God, who loved me and gave himself for me'* (Galatians 2:20). We are to *'imitate those who through faith and patience inherit what has been promised'* (Hebrews 6:12).

For example, God's word says he can and will forgive our sin, when we confess our sins.[5] He confirms his word to us by the work of his Holy Spirit, cleansing us, giving us a clear conscience, enabling us to move forward. We believe, therefore we act, in obedience to his word. *'Show me your faith without deeds, and I will show you my **faith** by **what I do'*** (James 2:18). Faith without deeds is useless.

As we walk in faith, that removes all false props we may have tried to depend on. This also discourages others from leaning on us in an ungodly, dependent way. Our dependence is in God and his word.

This is completely different from the world who walk according to their feelings, their sinful nature, their greed, and envy, or to meet their dependency needs or their need for approval. We act on God's word, believing God's word for us, and by doing so we begin to be led by God's Holy Spirit.

The enemy, or enemies, will always be trying to prevent us:
(a) from receiving from God, or trying to snatch God's word from us before it produces fruit in our lives;[6]
(b) by taking what God has given us;[7]

(c) from walking in the fullness of God's plan and purpose for our lives.

We are to hold onto God's promises for us. We are to imitate those *'who through faith and patience inherit what has been promised'* (Hebrews 6:12).[8]

When we walk by faith we believe God's word for us, however contrary to people's opinions the opposition that is put against us, or difficult the circumstances. We are not to listen to our negative emotions, we are to hold onto God's word for us. We receive and accept Jesus by faith. We accept his word for us by faith that he is able to forgive.[9] We then go on believing he is able to save completely.[10]

The more we believe, accept and act upon God's word in obedience, the more Spirit-filled we will be. The more we will reflect the nature and character of the Lord Jesus. We, as people, rise up and overcome as we walk by faith. We rise above events and circumstances. God's work is by faith (1 Timothy 1:4).

When we walk by faith our security is in Jesus and his word for us. We are dependent on him, his promises and his ability to hold, keep us and fulfil his plan for us. We stand on God's word for us. We act because we believe. The world will see the fruit from a faith-filled life, in the light.

Faithfulness is a fruit of God's Holy Spirit. A life full of faith in God; his ability, his enabling and his goodness. We are to overcome by persevering. We are secure in the knowledge of his ability to succeed for us. The enemy will try to limit God's people to their own human limits, our human strength, and ability, and our human reasoning. We are able to go beyond these because we have God's enabling and resources (his Holy Spirit and his word). We are to walk according to the Spirit which is a completely different way from walking in our natural strengths. When we walk by faith our potential is vast.

5. We walk as a people who have hope

The world has no hope. They are *'without hope and without God in the world'* (Ephesians 2:12). Our hope is in God. *'Some trust in chariots and some in horses, but we trust in the name of the Lord our God'* (Psalm 20:7–8). We have a hope of eternal life. We have a living hope.[11] We have an inheritance that can never perish, spoil or fade.[12] We have a hope of being saved, of salvation.[13] We have hope, Jesus is coming again.[14]

We need to know the hope to which we are called heavenward in Christ, *'that you may know the hope to which he has called you, the riches of his glorious inheritance in the saints'* (Ephesians 1:18). This hope motivates us. *'We continually remember before our God and Father your work produced by faith, your labour prompted by love, and your endurance inspired by hope in our Lord Jesus Christ'* (1 Thessalonians 1:3). Hope in itself is a light. People will seek the reason **for** our hope,[15] as we walk in the light.

6. We walk in obedience

'Whoever has my commands and obeys them, he is the one who loves me' (John 14:21). We are to walk in obedience to God's written word and his specific word for our lives.[16] We are not to be swayed by the opinions of men or to live for their approval. *'We know you are a man of integrity and that you teach the way of God in accordance with the truth'* (Matthew 22:16). *'Am I now trying to win the approval of men, or of God? Or am I trying to please men? If I were still trying to please men, I would not be a servant of Christ'* (Galatians 1:10). **When we honour God, he honours us**.

We walk in obedience to Jesus, his word and ways and not according to the world's standards or conforming to the traditions of men. We believe God's word for us and act on that word. The more in agreement (submitted) our lives are to the will and word of God, the more secure our lives.[17] *'His commands are not burdensome'* (1 John 5:3). **His** burden is easy and his yoke is light. It is when we either are doing the wrong thing, carrying negative emotions and suppressed darkness, or are walking in our own strength not relying on God's Holy Spirit, we become burdened. We are to build on **rock**, hearing God's word and putting that word into practice.[18] *'When the storm has swept by, the wicked are gone, but the righteous stand* *firm forever'* (Proverbs 10:25). Our obedience is the response of our love.[19]

This is totally different from people who are disobedient, who are involved in such things as sexual immorality, greed, selfish ambition, *'foolish talk or coarse joking.'* (Ephesians 5:3–4).[20] They may be motivated by money, power, fame, popularity, envy or greed. They do not listen to or hear God's word, they refuse to accept the truth and be saved.

We are not to waste our God-given ability, gifts and talents. We are to use them to the best of our ability.[21]

We are to *'Love the Lord your God with all your heart and with all your soul and with all your mind.'* This is the first and greatest command. The second is, *'Love your neighbour as yourselves'* (Matthew 22:37–39). As we walk in the good works prepared for us [22] **we give God glory**. We are to *'serve wholeheartedly, as if you were serving the Lord, not men, because you know that the Lord will reward everyone for whatever good he does'* (Ephesians 6:7). Obedience in itself allows God to act for us and defeat our enemies.[23] God's word clearly states that when we obey his commands our enemies will be defeated. As we obey and walk in obedience, so the natural consequence of that is defeat of our enemies.

We are to commit ourselves to our Creator God and to continue to do good, when opposed and persecuted, until God acts on our behalf against our enemies.[24]

The enemy will try to use our emotions to dominate, manipulate, control, to tempt us to walk outside God's will for us. Our choices during testing times are to be based on God's word for us. We are not to be enticed. We are to resist the enemy and he will flee from us. We are not to act on our emotions. Otherwise we may be 'led' by a negative emotion such as anxiety. A negative emotion such as anxiety may motivate us to follow the wrong course of action to try to get the security and peace we need. Peace, the fruit of God's Holy Spirit, is the right emotion from which to make choices, not anxiety. This is when our security is in Jesus.

Fear, another negative emotion, can wrongly motivate us. Fear of persecution, fear of failure. We need to be secure in the knowledge of God's love for us. Our motive is Jesus' love. Christ's love compels us because we have the knowledge of the depth of his love and forgiveness. We are called to overcome our negative emotions, not to be ruled by them. As we walk in step with God's Holy Spirit so our emotions are fruitful (they are in God's order).

People will see the fruit of our obedience. *'If you fully obey the Lord your God ... the Lord your God will set you high above all the nations on earth'* (Deuteronomy 28:1, 3). It is important we are seen to do the right actions. One of the main fruits of obedience is blessing. God is able to release his blessing. People will know we have a good God. *'All these blessing will come upon you and accompany you ... the Lord will send a blessing on everything you put your hand to'* (Deuteronomy 28:2, 8).[25] Our obedience enables God to answer our prayer. *'The prayer of a righteous man is powerful and effective'* (James 5:16). The fruit of that is vast. This promise is given in the context of walking in the light with one another. The world shall see that through our God we shall do great exploits.[26]

Obedience to God's word will enable us to overcome our enemies. We will be seen to be victorious. We will no longer be subject to our oppressors. We will end up walking in accordance to God's will and by the power of his Holy Spirit. God is able to change us, change our heart attitudes as we walk in obedience to his word, reflecting more of his nature.

Jesus loves obedience. There are some key areas of obedience:

(a) We are to put on the full armour of God.[27]

(b) We are to walk in forgiveness. Giving our forgiveness to others and receiving God's forgiveness for us.

(c) We are to love our enemies. Never to repay insult with insult but with blessing. We are to overcome evil with good. *'Do not be overcome by evil, but overcome evil with good'* (Romans 12:21). We can choose by the power of God's Holy Spirit, to forgive our enemies releasing them from any debt. It is God who will avenge. *'I will repay'* (Hebrews 10:30), says the Lord. *'It is a dreadful thing to fall into the hands of the living God'* (Hebrews 10:31), if they misuse or abuse our kindness, it is God himself who will work for us and act on our behalf. *'If you listen carefully to what he says and do all that I say, I will be an enemy to your enemies and will oppose those who oppose you'* (Exodus 23:22).

(d) We need to keep our heart-attitude pure.[28] We are not to use any forms of flattery or to show favouritism. We need to have clean hands and a pure heart in our dealings with people. *'Therefore, rid yourself of all malice and all deceit, hypocrisy, envy, and slander of every kind'* (1 Peter 2:1).

(e) We should be willing to help practically[29] the poor and those in any kind of need or under oppression. *'For he stands at the right hand of the needy one, to save his life from those who condemn him'* (Psalm 109:31). *'If you spend yourselves on behalf of the hungry and satisfy the needs of the oppressed, then your light will rise in the darkness, and your night will become like the noon day'* (Isaiah 58:10). We are a different people, our attitudes and values are different. They should be the result of and the working of our faith and love.

(f) Walking in the light: the light will show the fruit of obedience, a life walked in the light of love of Jesus. They will also see the way in which we handle and overcome in trials and temptation.

7. Avoidance of sin and related behaviour

'No-one who is born of God will continue to sin, because God's seed remains in him; he cannot go on sinning' (1 John 3:9). We are born of God. Children of God born of his Holy Spirit, will not go on sinning. We are no longer slaves to sin but slaves to righteousness[30] *'He who does what is sinful is of the devil'* (1 John 3:8).

The power of sin to hold us when we believe on the name of Jesus and accept him, is broken. This is because of the blood of Jesus and the victory of the cross. We have been born again, not of the sinful nature but born of God. God lives within us. Christ in you the hope of glory. If we do sin, not continually but are led stray, deceived, the blood of Jesus is able to cleanse us from all sin as we confess our sin.[31]

We are to put God's word into action. *'Even a child is* **known** *by his actions, by whether his conduct is pure and right'* (Proverbs 20:11). *'Anyone who does not do what is right is not a child of God; nor is anyone who does not love his brother'* (1 John 3:10).

It is God's grace and his goodness towards us, his love and his ability to save completely, that enables us to stop sinning. *'For the grace of God that brings salvation has appeared to all men. It teaches us to say "***No***" to ungodliness and worldly passions, and to live self-controlled, upright and godly lives'* (Titus 2:11–12).

We need to know that the promises God has given us are powerful. *'His divine power* **has given us** *everything we need for life and godliness through our knowledge of him who called us by his own glory and goodness. Through these he has given us his very great and precious promises, so that* **through them** *you may participate in the divine nature and escape the corruption in the world caused by evil desires'* (2 Peter 1:3–4).

We have no excuse to sin; we have God's Holy Spirit living in us, the same Spirit that raised Jesus from the dead. We can choose not to sin. We are promised we will not be tempted beyond that which we can bear. As children of God we are to walk in step with, and be led by, the Holy Spirit and not act on our sinful nature.

We are God's people, no longer under law but under grace. We acknowledge we need God's forgiveness, his love, his ability and his strength, his enabling. The Holy Spirit enables us to live up to all that God asks of us. God puts in our hearts new desires. *'His divine power has given us everything we need for life and godliness'* (2 Peter 1:3).

The world is still under the law, the dos, the don'ts, can'ts, shouldn'ts, rules and regulations. These can never deal with the sinful nature; to do this we need a new nature, God's nature within us.[32] We are a different people, the light will reveal us to be so.

God makes us new creations in him.[33] We need to fix our eyes on our future reward, our inheritance, so we do not give up in times of persecution, and opposition. *'So do not throw away your confidence; it will be richly rewarded. You need to persevere so that when you have done the will of God, you will receive what he has promised'* (Hebrews 10:35–36).

References

1. Romans 12:2; 1 Thessalonians 4:1
2. Hebrews 11:6; Colossians 3:24
3. Psalm 139:16; Ephesians 1:11; Jeremiah 29:11
4. 1 Peter 4:2
5. 1 John 1:9
6. Matthew 13:19
7. John 10:10
8. Psalm 138:8
9. 1 John 1:9; Acts 26:18
10. Hebrews 7:25
11. 1 Peter 1:3
12. 1 Peter 1:4
13. 1 Thessalonians 5:9; 1 Peter 1:9
14. 1 Thessalonians 4:16–17; 2 Thessalonians 1:7–10
15. 1 Peter 3:15–16
16. Romans 8:14
17. Matthew 7:24–25
18. Matthew 7:24
19. 1 John 2:5; John 14:21
20. Ephesians 2:1–3
21. Colossians 3:23–24; Matthew 25:21
22. Ephesians 2:10
23. Deuteronomy 28:7; Psalm 81:13–14
24. Hebrews 10:30–31; Romans 12:17–19
25. Deuteronomy 28:11–12; Malachi 3:10
26. Hebrews 11:33
27. Ephesians 6:11
28. Philippians 2:3–5; Matthew 20:25–26
29. James 2:14–17; 1 John 3:17–18
30. Romans 6:18, 22
31. 1 John 1:9; 2:1–2
32. John 1:12–13; 3:5–7
33. 2 Corinthians 5:17

Chapter 9

Our Behaviour

Our behaviour, the way we act, will show the world that we are the children of God. We belong to a living God and believe in the name of Jesus and follow him. There are particular aspects of our behaviour that show we are God's. We are his sheep: *'We are his people, the sheep of his pasture'* (Psalm 100:3). *'You are a chosen people, a royal priesthood, a holy nation, a people **belonging to God**, that you may declare the praises of him who **called you out of darkness into his wonderful light'** (1 Peter 2:9). *'All the peoples on earth will see that you are called by the name of the Lord, and they will fear you'* (Deuteronomy 28:10).

People will recognize us by the fruit that we bear. It is to God's glory that we bear much fruit showing ourselves to be his disciples.[1] *'By their fruit you will recognize them'* (Matthew 7:20). We know that no good tree bears bad fruit and no bad tree bears good fruit. Our fruit may be the fruit of the Spirit,[2] our good works,[3] our behaviour, genuine lasting relationships based on Jesus, for the good of others. There will be both lasting fruits[4] and eternal reward. It is so important that we recognize God's people, the work of his Holy Spirit, and discern correctly the enemy's 'works'. We need to be in the light. We need to be clean on the inside to bear good fruit, to be visible.

Aspects of our behaviour that show we are God's

1. Our love

Our love *for our Creator God*

Jesus said, *'If God were your Father, you would love me'* (John 8:42). *'Whoever has my commands and obeys them, he is the one who loves me'* (John 14:20–21). The world's concept of 'love' is very different from God's. Love that clings, grasps, depends on and draws from others, and seeks its own end does not come from God. *'For God so loved the world that he gave his one and only Son, that whoever believes in him shall not perish but have eternal life'* (John 3:16). God's love **for** us which he has poured into our hearts[5] enables us to stand and to give. Jesus laid down his life **for** us. *'Everyone who loves has been born of God and knows God'* (1 John 4:7). The first command is this: To love the Lord your God with all your heart, soul and strength; the second is this: To love your neighbour as yourself. We are not to make the mistake of loving people before or 'more' than God, letting them take his rightful place in our lives. We are to love the Lord first, and from that love, love others. We will be defeated by our enemies if we love them more or put people before God. This is because there are so many areas of people's lives that are not yet submitted to the Lordship of Jesus. These areas (there may be demonic interference, and unconfessed sin) will stand in opposition to God, his ways, his plans and purpose for us and others' lives. They will try to manipulate us into compromising our faith to make us lukewarm.

Our love *for each other*

If we belong to God, we will obey his commands. *'Whoever loves his brother lives in the light, and there is nothing in him to make him stumble. But whoever hates his brother is in darkness'* (1 John 2:10–11).[6] *'Let us not love with words or tongue but with actions and in truth'* (1 John 3:18). We are to love in our actions. *'If anyone has material possessions and sees his brother in need but has no pity on him, how can the love of God be in him?'* (1 John 3:17). *'Do not be like Cain, who belonged to the evil one and murdered his brother. And why ... Because his own actions were evil and his brother's righteous'* (1 John 3:12).

We are to love one another genuinely from our hearts,[7] to want their good, to want them to succeed and be honoured. There is a depth to our love, a faithfulness. *'Above all, love each other deeply, because love covers over a multitude of sins'* (1 Peter 4:8). Our love isn't to be dependent on events and circumstances.

Our love *for our enemies*

We are to overcome evil with good. *'But I tell you: Love your enemies and pray for those who persecute you, that you may be sons of your Father in heaven ... If you love those who love you, what reward will you get?'* (Matthew 5:44–46). We are not to hold anything against our enemies, in the knowledge that as long as we forgive they cannot harm us or God's plan for our lives. Jesus died for them, and his will is that they should not perish but come to a saving knowledge of himself.

In the knowledge we belong to God, he will **not** allow an enemy of God to touch or harm us beyond that which God can work for our good. If they persist in evil, he will act against them and on our behalf.[8] We are to overcome evil with good and to bless those who both insult and persecute us. *'Do not be overcome by evil, but overcome evil with good'* (Romans 12:21).

This love is totally alien to people in the world who return hate for hate, insult for insult. *'If you love those who love you, what reward will you get? ... And, if you greet only your brothers, what are you doing more than others?'* (Matthew 5:46–47).[9] The light will reveal who we are, sons and daughters of the living God.

We are overcomers. *'For everyone born of God overcomes the world. This is the victory that has overcome the world, even our faith. Who is it that overcomes the world? Only he who believes that Jesus is the Son of God'* (1 John 5:4–5). We overcome our enemies as we forgive and bless them.[10] *'If your enemy is* hungry, give him food to eat; if he is thirsty, give him water to drink. In doing this, you will heap burning coals on his head, and the Lord will reward you' (Proverbs 25:21–22). We lose if we retaliate or become resentful and bitter. God will avenge and repay. *'Do not take revenge, my friends, but leave room for God's wrath, for it is written: It is mine to avenge;* **I will repay**, *says the Lord'* (Romans 12:19). *'It is a dreadful thing to fall into the hands of the living God'* (Hebrews 10:31). *'The face of the Lord is against those who do evil'* (1 Peter 3:12). We are told that no weapon that is fashioned against us will stand, and that sinners will not stand [11] in the assembly of the righteous.[12]

2. Our unity

Jesus prayed, *'May they be brought to complete unity* **to let the world know that you sent me and have loved them** *even as you have loved me'* (John 17:23). *'May the God who gives endurance and encouragement,* **give you a spirit of unity** *among yourselves as you follow Christ Jesus'* (Romans 15:5).

There is a unity of the Spirit. We belong to each other. We are children of God, *'born not of natural descent, nor of human decision, or a husband's will, but born of God'* (John 1:13). We cannot understand God's word and spiritual truths except **by the Holy Spirit**. They are spiritually discerned. God's Spirit leads us into all truth.[13] *'The man without the Spirit does not accept the things that come from the Spirit of God, for they are foolishness to him, and he cannot understand them, because they are spiritually discerned'* (1 Corinthians 2:14). Those who know God accept and believe his words, which are Spirit and life.[14]

'We have not received the spirit of the world but the Spirit who is from God, that we may understand what God has freely given us' (1 Corinthians 2:12).

The Holy Spirit, the Spirit of God, gives us a unity. Those who are led by the Spirit are sons of God. We are to keep in step with God's Holy Spirit, not gratify the sinful nature. If we walk in step with the Holy Spirit there will be a unity. *'There are different kinds of gifts, but* **the same Spirit**. *There are different kinds of service,* **but the same Lord**. *There are different kinds of* *working, but **the same God** works...'* (1 Corinthians 12:4–6). Unity does not mean conformity.

We are his people. We recognize God's voice, and we recognize him. There is an inner knowing, recognizing of his voice and his work. *'My sheep listen to my voice. I know them, and they follow me'* (John 10:27). The world doesn't know or accept God's Holy Spirit, his leading and guidance.

To stay in unity we need to:

(a) **stay** close to God's word which is the truth. *'All scripture is God-breathed and is useful for teaching, rebuking, correcting and training in righteousness'* (2 Timothy 3:16).

(b) continually ask the Lord to teach us his ways.[15]

(c) be filled with the Holy Spirit.

(d) know God has **no favourites**.

We belong to another. *'**No** more boasting about men! **All** things are yours, whether Paul or Apollos or Cephas, or the world or life ... all are yours, and you are of Christ, and Christ is of God'* (1 Corinthians 3:21–23). This removes any grounds for envy or jealousy. We need to concentrate on what we have been given, and to use our gifts.

3. God's people will not try to kill

'Anyone who hates his brother is a murderer, and you know that no murderer has eternal life in him' (1 John 3:15). *'The thief comes only to steal and kill and destroy. I have come that they may have life, and have it to the full'* (John 10:10). Spiritual truths are spiritually discerned.

The enemy will try to rob and steal. He will try to destroy the person to whom a gift has been given and then try to take their gift.[16] **No-one can snatch us from God's hand.** *'No-one can snatch them out of my hand. My Father, who has given them to me, is greater than all; no-one can snatch them out of my Father's hand'* (John 10:28–29).

They tried to kill Jesus, but death had no hold on him – he defeated his enemy death[17] and rose from the dead and is now seated at the right hand of God. *'God exalted him to the highest place and gave him the name that is above every name'* (Philippians 2:9). We are in Jesus.

- We have been given the gift of eternal life.[18] You can't earn it or take it from another. Jesus will in no way cast away or reject anyone who goes to him.
- We have been given our inheritance that can never perish, spoil or fade.[19]
- We have the deposit of God's Holy Spirit guaranteeing what is to come. He has set his seal of ownership on us (2 Corinthians 1:22).[20]
- *'Do not be afraid, little flock, for your Father has been pleased to give you the kingdom'* (Luke 12:32). Jesus loves us. He chose to give good gifts to us.

As children of God we are secure in the knowledge of his love for us, his goodness towards us:

(a) we know we have been given glorious riches in Christ;

(b) we know we do not have to take or steal; because

(c) we know our heavenly Father is the rewarder of those who earnestly seek him. *'No good thing does he withhold from those whose walk is blameless'* (Psalm 84:11);

(d) we know God's nature is to give.[21] **'I will do whatever you ask in my name'** (John 14:13–14).[22]

Our nature as his people, is to choose to bless, to give, to uphold, to forgive. We reflect his nature.

It can be a trial to believe that God will reward each person according to what they have done, when we see the enemy seemingly prosper. We can go on to defeat our enemies **if** we keep on persevering, **believing God will reward**[23] **us. God will fulfil his promises to us.**[24] Our lives are to stay sweet.

The enemy has no such hope,[25] no such inheritance. If someone is trying to take or steal from you, you can be sure **that is not the work of God's Holy Spirit**. That is the enemy. They do not know God and his ways. *'All the ways of the Lord are loving and faithful for those who keep the demands of his covenant'* (Psalm 25:10).

If we are born of God's Holy Spirit, then I believe God plants in us the desire to see people built up. We hate the devil, his destructiveness, *'hate what is evil; cling to what is good'* (Romans 12:9). Jesus came to destroy the works of the devil.[26] *'The reason the Son of God appeared was to destroy the devil's work'* (1 John 3:8). Simply by persevering in doing good, we have the light of the world in us, we push back the powers of darkness.

4. We walk in *truth*

We walk in the truth of God's word.[27] We are **for** the truth.[28] God's people, those who belong to Jesus, love and hold in high regard the truth. **The truth** is important. Jesus said: *'I am the way and the truth and the life'* (John 14:6). Jesus is the truth. He is the word of God made flesh.[29] God's word is the truth. It is the truth of the gospel that will set people free into *'the glorious freedom of the children of God'* (Romans 8:21).[30] We are saved because we believe the truth.[31] People perish because they do not love, believe, or want the truth. *'They perish because they refuse to **love** the truth and so be saved'* (2 Thessalonians 2:10).

The devil is a liar and the 'father' of lies. There is **no** truth in him. *'When he lies, he speaks his native language, for he is a liar'* (John 8:44). If we say we have fellowship, and are in relationship with God yet do not walk in the light, we lie. We are not living in truth.[32]

When you hear anyone oppose God's word – speak contrary to scripture, that is a lie, the work of the enemy, deathly destruction. People can also lie about their behaviour concerning events, denying the truth. That is of the enemy. God's word is God's authority for us. God's authority is greater than any other authority (John 10:29). He has exalted above all things his name and his word.

We have authority and power over our enemy when we speak the truth. God's word is sharper than any two-edged sword. God's word is the truth [33] and gives light. *'Your word is a lamp to my feet and a light for my path'* (Psalm 119:105). God is on our side when we speak the truth.[34] *'If God is for us, who can be against us? ... Who will bring any charge against those whom God has chosen?'* (Romans 8:31, 33). When we speak the truth God will affirm us, confirming the truth of his word. God's word is the sword of the Spirit.[35] The 'belt of truth' [36] is also part of the armour of God. The devil's aim is to put you down, and speaking the truth defeats him.[37] God's word will reveal truth from error, light from darkness, a pure heart from a corrupt one.[38] *'Do not add to his words, or he will rebuke you and prove you a liar'* (Proverbs 30:6).

If we:

(a) claim to be without sin, there is no truth in us;[39]

(b) say we love God but hate our brother, we lie;[40]

(c) say we know God (Jesus) but do not do what he says, we also lie![41]

(d) claim we are in relationship with God yet walk in darkness, we lie.[42]

When we believe and **act** on the truth of God's word, agreeing with what God says, and not the enemy, we begin to walk as Jesus did. We get the **victory** over the devil's schemes. We need to believe in our heart, *'see to it, brothers, that none of you has a sinful, unbelieving heart'* (Hebrews 3:12).

'A lying tongue hates those it hurts and a flattering mouth works ruin' (Proverbs 26:28). People who are wicked **suppress** the truth (Romans 1:18). This shows how destructive people are when they speak lies. *'If a ruler listens to lies, all his officials become wicked'* (Proverbs 29:12). Jesus said, *'For this I came into the world to testify to the truth. Everyone on the side of truth listens to me'* (John 18:37). A truthful person saves lives. *'A false witness will perish. Whoever listens to him will be destroyed'* (Proverbs 21:28). If our hearts are clean on the inside and we speak the truth of God's word,[43] our enemy and the darkness are defeated. Our light will shine. We will overcome and be seen to do so.

5. We walk in *forgiveness*

When we walk both receiving God's forgiveness and extending his and **our** forgiveness to others, it is powerful. We need to learn to walk in forgiveness. We are not a people who retaliate or hold grudges. Our God is on the throne. When we walk in forgiveness, the enemy cannot harm us or prevent God's purpose for our lives being fulfilled.

There is no quicker way to be defeated by our enemies than if we don't forgive. We will be utterly defeated. We walk outside God's protection for us. We walk in condemnation, if we do not learn to forgive. We are clearly told that if we do not forgive other people's sins, ours will not be forgiven. *'For if you forgive men when they sin against you, your heavenly Father will also forgive you. But if you do not forgive men their sins, your Father will not forgive your sins'* (Matthew 6:14–15).[44]

Our forgiveness opens the door to heaven for ourselves (heaven on earth!), and for others. A forgiven life is a beautiful life reflecting God's nature, his mercy and the joy of being forgiven and in relationship. *'For he has rescued us from the dominion of darkness and brought us into the Kingdom of the Son he loves, in whom we have redemption, the forgiveness of sins'* (Colossians 1:13).

When we forgive

(a) The enemy has no grounds to accuse or condemn.[45] *'For the accuser of our brothers, who accuses them before our God day and night, has been hurled down. They overcame him by the blood of the Lamb and by the word of their testimony'* (Revelation 12:10–11).

(b) The Lord will forgive you.[46] The enemy will not be able to put you down. *'No weapon forged against you will prevail, and you will refute every tongue that accuses you'* (Isaiah 54:17). *'If you, O Lord, kept a record of sins, O Lord, who could stand? But with you there is forgiveness; therefore you are feared'* (Psalm 130:3–4).[47] Sinners will not stand in the assembly of the righteous.[48]

(c) It allows room for God's wrath. *'It is mine to avenge; I will repay, and again, ... The Lord will judge his people. It is a dreadful thing to fall into the hands of the living God'* (Hebrews 10:30–31).[49] We humanly cannot defeat our enemies. that is for God to **act** on our behalf as we choose to walk in forgiveness. If we do not forgive we come under God's judgement and wrath as well, and not his grace.

(d) I believe God's forgiveness and our ability to forgive opens up the gate for us to walk in God's anointing for us. It is the prayer of a righteous man or woman that is powerful and effective.[50]

(e) It enables God to release his plan and purpose for our lives. The only way the enemy can prevent God's plan and purpose for our lives to bear much fruit, is when we refuse to forgive a person. We literally block the way forward. As soon as we forgive, the way opens up for us.

(f) We will be the aroma of Christ. *'For we are to God the aroma of Christ among those who are being saved and those who are perishing'* (2 Corinthians 2:14–16). A forgiven life makes a beautiful person, with the desire to forgive, and lift others up. We are just so grateful to have been forgiven.[51]

(g) Our forgiveness and ability to forgive will enable us to walk in victory. Victory over our circumstances. Victory over those who would pull us down. There is nothing in us to make others stumble;[52] as we walk in forgiveness in the light.

When we do not forgive, walking in the light, we cause others to stumble. Our forgiveness will bring into our lives the reality that *'in all things God works for the good of those who love him'* (Romans 8:28). Forgiveness is a choice, the enemy will try to deceive us that we need to feel like forgiving, or that we need to want to forgive, or will tempt us to listen to all the feelings of hate, anger, resentment and bitterness, so we feel we can't possibly forgive. We feel hypocritical to forgive, we are not being true to our feelings! The enemy will try to stir up every negative feeling and hate, to try to make us retaliate.

We are to overcome our feelings **by an act of our will**, choosing to forgive. We can forgive, we have Christ within us, his grace within us which enables us to forgive. When we are wronged, or we perceive we have been, if we do not forgive, we will be defeated until we forgive those we have hurt us. We need to know God is **for** us.[53]

6. We care about the poor and justice for the oppressed

The righteous care about justice[54] for the poor. *'When justice is done, it brings joy to the righteous but terror to evil doers'* (Proverbs

86

21:15). *'I know that the Lord secures justice for the poor and upholds the cause of the needy'* (Psalm 140:12).[55] *'For he stands at the right hand of the needy one, to save his life from those who condemn him'* (Psalm 109:31). The wicked condemn the innocent, and acquit the guilty if there is selfish gain. We are not to fear people's intimidations and threats. *'Acquitting the guilty and condemning the innocent – the Lord detests'* (Proverbs 17:15).

Our concerns, cares, motives and desires as God's people, are totally different from those who are without hope and without God in the world.[56] We have the knowledge of God's loving kindness and care. We are to extend that same concern, love and care, practically.

'Blessed is he who has regard for the weak; the Lord delivers him in times of trouble ... and not surrender him to the desire of his foes' (Psalm 41:1–2).[57]

It is so easy to be driven by the enemy, by our emotions and feelings. There are some things that the enemy will not want us to do. He will not want us to care for the poor, to lift the hurting or the oppressed, to secure justice for them. He will not want us to succeed in helping the weak and the oppressed. He will oppose us as we seek to obey the Lord and his guiding.

Our concern for justice for the oppressed and those in need will have a practical outworking.[58] Our right heart-motive for securing justice for the poor, is important. You can be sure if our heart-motive is wrong (if we are in for gain, favour or approval) the enemy will be able to undermine and defeat our 'good' plan. He will cause us to give up. We need to hear God and act in faith on his word. We need a word of faith. If God has spoken to us concerning a vision, a good work,[59] God will accomplish his plan. *'It is God who works in you to will and to act according to his good purpose'* (Philippians 2:13). We are to persevere until the goal, dream or vision has been fulfilled. Our heart-motive needs to be in line with God's. If we allow God to work in us by his Holy Spirit, he will refine our heart-motive as we walk in faith and obedience. We can ask for the heart of God in any given situation.

We are to *'speak up for those who cannot speak for themselves, for the rights of all who are destitute. Speak up and judge fairly, defend the rights of the poor and needy'* (Proverbs 31:8–9).

We need to realize the impact when God's justice prevails. When we are either given justice or act justly. *'When justice is done, it brings **joy** to the righteous but terror to evildoers'* (Proverbs 21:15). *'When the righteous triumph there is great elation'* (Proverbs 28:12). We are to defend the rights of the poor and needy.[60] God is a God of justice.[61] *'Even a child is known by his actions, whether his conduct is pure and right'* (Proverbs 20:11).

We need to have a clean hand and a pure heart, otherwise we will become hypocritical, if we are not clean, and our inner values and motives are not godly.[62] We need to walk in the light personally.

We will **never** defeat our enemies if we ourselves plunder the poor, or defraud those who work for us, or try to gain wealth unjustly (Proverbs 11:18), or even defraud those over us in authority. We will become an enemy ourselves. We are to commit ourselves to our Creator God and continue to do good. *'Who is going to harm you if you are eager to do good? But even if you should suffer for what is right, you are blessed'* (1 Peter 3:13).[63]

We have a lovely promise of God's guidance, and that our light will shine, as we act on behalf of those in need. *'And if you spend yourselves on behalf of the hungry and satisfy the needs of the oppressed, **then your light will rise in the darkness and your light will become like the noonday. The Lord will guide you** always; he will satisfy your needs . . . '* (Isaiah 58:10–11).

References

1. John 15:8
2. Galatians 5:22–23
3. Ephesians 2:10; James 2:15–18; 1 John 3:17–18
4. John 15:16; Matthew 13:23
5. Romans 5:5
6. 1 John 4:11–12
7. Romans 12:9–10; 1 Corinthians 13:1–8
8. Exodus 23:22; Romans 8:31; 12:19; Isaiah 54:17
9. Matthew 5:44

10. Romans 12:17–18, 21; 1 Peter 3:9
11. Isaiah 54:17
12. Psalm 1:5
13. John 14:16–17, 25–26; 16:13
14. John 6:63; 8:47
15. Psalm 25:4–5, 8–9, 12
16. Matthew 21:38–43
17. 1 Corinthians 15:25–26, 54–57
18. Romans 6:23
19. 1 Peter 1:3–4
20. Ephesians 1:13–14
21. Malachi 3:10; Luke 6:38
22. John 15:16
23. Hebrews 10:35–36
24. 2 Corinthians 1:20
25. Ephesians 2:12
26. 1 John 3:8
27. 3 John 3
28. 2 Corinthians 13:8
29. John 1:1–2, 14
30. John 8:31–32; Romans 8:21
31. 2 Thessalonians 2:13–15
32. 1 John 1:6
33. John 17:17
34. Psalm 45:4; 51:6; Proverbs 12:19
35. Ephesians 6:17
36. Ephesians 6:14
37. Psalm 15:2–5; Ephesians 6:13–14; Romans 10:9
38. Hebrews 4:12–13
39. 1 John 1:8–10; 2:1–2
40. 1 John 4:19–21
41. 1 John 2:4
42. 1 John 1:6
43. Ephesians 6:17
44. Matthew 18:32–35
45. 1 John 1:9; 1 Corinthians 15:3
46. 2 Corinthians 5:21; Matthew 6:14–15
47. Psalm 55:22
48. Psalm 1:5
49. Romans 12:19
50. James 5:16
51. Luke 7:42–48
52. 1 John 2:10
53. Romans 8:31
54. Deuteronomy 16:19–20
55. Isaiah 25:4; Proverbs 24:23–25
56. Ephesians 2:12
57. Psalm 82:3–4
58. James 2:14–16; 1 John 3:17
59. Ephesians 2:10; 2 Thessalonians 1:11

60. Proverbs 31:8–9
61. Proverbs 21:3; Micah 6:8
62. Matthew 23:28
63. 1 Peter 4:14–16

Chapter 10

By Our Speech

Letting our light shine by what we say

The only person who can defeat our enemy is the Lord Jesus Christ by the power of his Holy Spirit. We live in him, so we also will get the victory and defeat our enemies by the power of the Holy Spirit. We can defeat and get the victory over our enemies by walking by faith [1] in obedience, living in accordance with God's word, walking in the light. As we let our light shine, speaking the truth, we will be seen to be the winners, those who overcome.[2]

A powerful testimony causes people to assess their own lives and values. This enables them to ask questions and to make informed choices. People need to hear God's word, the truth, to enable them to believe and to come to a saving knowledge of Jesus, *'How, then, can they call on the one they have not believed in? And how can they believe in the one of whom they have not heard? And how can they hear without someone preaching to them?'* (Romans 10:14).

'Consequently, faith comes from hearing the messages, and the message is heard through the word of Christ' (Romans 10:17). God's word is the foundation (Jesus is the word made flesh) of what we believe and what we do. We are to put God's word into practice. We need to hear God's word, his written and prophetic word for us.

The power of the spoken word

God's word is powerful and effective, able to heal, saves lives and accomplishes that which it was sent for.[3] God's words are:

(a) Spirit and life (John 6:63). *'If you confess with your mouth, "Jesus is Lord", and believe in your heart that God raised him from the dead,* **you** *will be saved'* (Romans 10:9);

(b) sharper than any two-edged sword and will penetrate our thoughts and heart-motives;[4]

(c) the truth.[5] *'Your word is a lamp to my feet and* **a light for** **my path'** (Psalm 119:105),[6] helping us to avoid deception and error;

(d) made flesh in Jesus[7] who is the word of God, and **the light of the world.**[8] *'I am the light of the world, whoever follows me will never walk in darkness'* (John 8:12);

(e) will accomplish[9] that for which it was sent. We are to be seen to be those who speak the truth.

Jesus is the way, the truth and the life.[10] The gospel is the **gospel of truth**.

(a) It is important that we speak the truth. *'A truthful witness saves lives'* (Proverbs 14:25).

(b) It is important that we speak the truth of God's word. Anything that is spoken that contradicts scripture, is of the enemy. Even when we do not 'feel' the truth, we are to speak in accordance with the truth.

Intimidation by our enemies

Our enemies will try to intimidate us[11] not to speak the truth. They know the truth of God's word and a truthful testimony will both expose and defeat them. The devil *'was a murderer from the beginning, not holding to the truth, for there is no truth in him. When he lies, he speaks his native language, for he is a liar'* (John 8:44).

They will try to:

(a) belittle us. They will try to undermine our faith by belittling or contradicting God's word. They would have us believe that the truth is of no value;

(b)   undermine our self-confidence;

(c)   persecute us because our words condemn them.

'For out of the overflow of the heart the mouth speaks. The good man brings good things out of the good stored up in him, and the evil man ... evil things' (Matthew 12:34–35). We will be accountable for what we say. *'For by your words you will be acquitted, and by your words you will be condemned'* (Matthew 12:37).

Whoever acknowledges Jesus before men, will themselves be acknowledged before God. That is a victory; every time we acknowledge God, he acknowledges us. The enemy does not want God's people to be acknowledged at all for the good they do, let alone before the throne of Grace.

So often I nearly give up and yet because I have scripture stored in my heart, *'I have hidden your word in my heart that I might not sin against you'* (Psalm 119:11) I speak the truth of God's word despite the sometimes difficult, seemingly impossible circumstances, and however weak I am in faith, God's word works and fights for me. God's word is the truth. God's word works for us.[12] We need to have a knowledge of God's word. God's word has been, with the name of Jesus, exalted above all things. God's word stands firm. When we speak the truth we have authority over our enemies and their lies.

They began to argue with Stephen, *'but they could not stand up against his wisdom or the Spirit by whom he spoke'* (Acts 6:10).[13]

We need to be very controlled in what we say. We need a tight reign on our tongue. A fruit of the Spirit is self-control. Our words can heal or hurt, lift up or pull down. They can give life. *'The tongue has the power of life and death'* (Proverbs 18:21).

In speech people are often careless, making comments like, 'You're useless'. We need to agree with God in our speech concerning others and ourselves. No, you are *'fearfully and wonderfully made'* (Psalm 139:14). Or, 'Oh, you're just a dreamer.' You're not just a dreamer. *'It is God who works in you, to will and to act according to his good purpose'* (Philippians 2:13).

And, *'without vision people cast off restraint'* (Proverbs 29:18). It is good and motivating to have dreams, goals and ambitions to work towards.

If we are to defeat our enemy we need to speak the truth. 'Silence' is an unwritten acceptance of the lie which, if not combated, can harm. Do not just not accept the lie, speak the truth of God's word immediately against the lie. Not only will that negative word not be able to harm and hurt you, it prevents any bitterness and resentment that those words can cause. It prevents the enemy getting any foothold, in trying to undermine our value, our self-worth, who we are in Jesus and our abilities. Again, negative, lying words are dangerous. Counteract them with the truth of God's word. People cannot challenge the truth which is God's word.[14]

Jesus spoke the truth to save, and sometimes to warn people. He never tried to prevent people fulfilling good goals. He wants us to shine. We are a people of truth. We are to speak the truth, loving others, and building them up.[15] Our words can create. When we speak the truth we take our stand against the devil's schemes. We are to overcome evil with good, darkness with light. What we say is a powerful weapon for good. We need to walk in the light concerning who we are and what we believe.

How God's words work for us

1. God's word can bring healing

God's word is creative, it can bring emotional and physical healing. *'The tongue that brings healing is a tree of life'* (Proverbs 15:4). *'The tongue of the wise brings healing'* (Proverbs 12:18). We can speak the truth into people's lives. That word will create where there has been damage and emotional hurt. We are to speak the truth from our heart (Psalm 15:2). We can be set free. *'Then you will know the truth, and the truth will set you free'* (John 8:32).

We can literally speak physical healing into people's lives. Peter said: *'In the name of Jesus of Nazareth, walk.'* He walked. It is *'by faith in the name of Jesus, and ... the faith that comes through him, that has given this complete healing to him'* (Acts 3:16). People were healed, as they responded to Jesus' words. To the paralysed man he said, *'Get up, take your mat and go home'* (Luke 5:24). He got up and walked, taking his mat and going home![16] The power of the spoken word. We can speak in Jesus' name. People will take notice. We have authority, a God-given authority. Jesus taught with authority[17] – his words and deeds matched.

2. We can deliver by the spoken word

(a) **From our fears**: God's word builds confidence.[18] We can call on the name of the Lord and ask him to deliver us. *'I sought the Lord, and he answered me; he delivered me from all my fears'* (Psalm 34:4).[19] We can confess the truth which builds up, and separates, in our emotions and heart, and in our understanding; truth from error.[20] God's word is truth and can penetrate deep within our spirits.

(b) **From deception**: *'Rescue me from deceitful and wicked men'* (Psalm 43:1). God's words are truth.[21] We can be deceived by other people's flattery, more often by our emotions, especially if we are being tempted. If our emotions and desires appear to contradict God's word, **agree with and act on his word**. If an ongoing situation, an unresolved situation, we can bring any word, any situation to God and ask for wisdom,[22] ask that his will prevail. Let him work by his Spirit. We are to pray.[23] We have the Spirit of truth in us. God's word is truth and it is light. It will expose, as we speak the truth, the lies and deception of the enemy. As we speak and live in God's truth, so the evil deeds of those who speak with evil intent, will be exposed.

(c) **From trouble**: We are to call upon the name of the Lord in trouble and he will deliver us. *'Call upon me in the day of trouble; I will deliver you, and you will honour me'* (Psalm 50:15). *'He will call upon me, and I will answer him; I will be with him in trouble, I will deliver him and honour him. With long life will I satisfy him'* (Psalm 91:15–16).[24]

(d) **From our enemies**: *'I will call to the Lord, who is worthy of praise, and I am saved from my enemies'* (2 Samuel 22:4).[25] *'And everyone who calls on the name of the Lord will be saved'* (Acts 2:21).[26] *'If you confess with your mouth, "Jesus is Lord", and believe in your heart that God raised him from the dead, you will be saved'* (Romans 10:9).

We are to call upon our Lord when in danger. Speaking the truth of God's word can deliver us from deadly perils, and prevent wrong behaviour patterns, in which the enemy tries to trap the righteous.

(e) **From demonic influences and forces**: Jesus delivered people with a word because of his authority, and his relationship with his heavenly Father.[27] Jesus has authority to deliver. **In Jesus' name**; as we submit to him and his authority so we are given authority to deliver. Deliverance is direct confrontation between the kingdom of darkness and the Kingdom of light. *'The seventy-two returned with joy and said, "Lord, even the demons submit to us in your name." He replied, "I saw satan fall like lightening from heaven. **I have given you authority** to trample on snakes and scorpions and to **overcome all the power of the enemy**; nothing will harm you. However, do not rejoice that the spirits submit to you, but rejoice that your names are written in heaven"'* (Luke 10:17–23).

We need to speak God's word. God's word is his authority for us. As we have walked in the light and let the light of Jesus, and the truth of the gospel, shine into our lives, so our light will, by the power of God's Holy Spirit expose demonic forces. We ourselves need to be submitted to God's word, his authority, and be in a place of forgiveness towards others, and having received God's forgiveness towards us, as we have walked in the light. We are to take our stand against the devil's schemes by speaking the truth. We can move forward into enemy territory as we speak the truth of God's word.

The disciples Paul and Barnabas, spoke the word of God **boldly**[28] for the Lord, who confirmed the message of his grace by enabling them to do miraculous signs and wonders.

God will confirm his word for us, the truth of what we say. He will affirm us. He will also expose the enemy, and his lies.

3. God's word sustains

*'The Sovereign Lord has given me an instructed tongue, to know the word that **sustains the weary**'* (Isaiah 50:4). When we speak God's word God works by his word; sustaining, upholding, and encouraging both us, and the person to whom we speak. *'The Son is the radiance of God's glory and the exact representation of his being, **sustaining all things by his powerful word**'* (Hebrews 1:3).

4. God's words bring comfort and encouragement

'Praise be to the God and Father of our Lord Jesus Christ, the Father of compassion and the God of all comfort, who comforts us in all our troubles, so that we can comfort those in any trouble with the comfort we ourselves have received from God' (2 Corinthians 1:3–7). We can encourage [29] one another with God's word, in the knowledge that God's word is the truth and builds up.[30] *'Therefore encourage one another and build each other up'* (1 Thessalonians 5:11).

5. God's word saves

*'The word is near you; it is in your mouth and in your heart, that is, the word of faith we are proclaiming: that if you **confess** with your mouth, "Jesus is Lord", and believe in your heart that God raised him from the dead, you will be saved'* (Romans 10:8–9).[31] We believe the truth, the gospel of truth and are saved.[32] We are to accept *'the word planted in you, which can save'* (James 1:21). We are made clean.[33] **God's word purifies.**

*'Consequently, **faith comes through hearing** the message, and the message is heard through the word of Christ'* (Romans 10:17). God's spoken word brings faith. *'I am not ashamed of the gospel, because it is the power of God for the salvation of everyone who believes'* (Romans 1:16).

6. God's words bear fruit

'But the one who received the seed that fell on good soil is the man

who hears the word and understands it. He produces a crop, yielding a hundred, sixty, or thirty times what was sown' (Matthew 13:23). That is how we initially enter the Kingdom of God. We believed the word of truth which was spoken to us. We then accepted and believed on the name of Jesus. Our walk with God is then continually hearing, believing and acting on the truth of God's spoken word.

God's work is by faith (1 Timothy 1:4). We are to live and walk by faith. *'Imitate those who through faith and patience inherit what has been promised'* (Hebrews 6:12). There is a righteousness that comes by faith.[34] It is by faith we overcome the world. *'For everyone born of God overcomes the world. This is the victory that has overcome the world, even our faith'* (1 John 5:4).

The more we speak God's word as part of our conversation, the more we'll overcome the darkness. God's words are Spirit and life. They expose the darkness, the lies, the hate of which people may not even be aware in their lives, enabling people to confess and repent. The more we have a knowledge of God's word, the more we have ourselves submitted to the light and have overcome, by speaking the truth into our lives, the more our light will shine in us and through us. The more we will overcome and be overcomers, as we go into any new, given situation. The battle begins in our lives. The more ground we have claimed for Jesus in our lives, the more of his love we will be able to bring into other people's lives and circumstances.

We need to listen to the truth

'He who belongs to God hears what God says. The reason you do not hear is, that you do not belong to God' (John 8:47). *'My sheep listen to my voice ... and they follow me'* (John 10:27).[35] *'I tell you the truth, whoever **hears** my word and believes him who sent me has eternal life'* (John 5:24). *'Everyone who listens to the Father and learns from him comes to me'* (John 6:45).

We are also told that if people listen to us, they are accepting Jesus' words, just as when we accept Jesus' word, we are accepting God. *'He who listens to you listens to me; he who rejects you rejects me; but he who rejects me rejects him who sent me'* (Luke 10:16).[36]

We need also to obey the truth

'Do not merely listen to the word, and so deceive yourselves. Do what it says' (James 1:22). As we ask the Lord to teach us and listen to him, *'wisdom will enter your heart and knowledge will be pleasant to our soul'* (Proverbs 2:10).[37]

Reasons why we need to store God's word in our hearts

(a) That we might not sin. *'I have hidden your word in my heart that I might not sin against you'* (Psalm 119:11).
(b) Out of the overflow of our hearts the mouth speaks. If we are full of the light of God's word, we will be able to speak the truth. We will also know how to answer people.[38]
(c) God's word works in us.[39] God's words change and purify us. *'Now you have purified yourselves by obeying the truth'* (1 Peter 1:22).
(d) God's word brings faith.

We are to live in accordance with what we speak. Our lives should be submitted to, and in line with, the word of God. To confess the truth we need to have stored God's word in our hearts. We can confess with our mouths to overcome discouragement and negative emotions or events.

- We can confess: *'I know that God is working all things together for the good of those who love him and have been called according to his purpose'* (Romans 8:28).
- We can confess: *'You intended to harm me but God intended it for good to accomplish what is now being done, the saving of many lives'* (Genesis 50:20).
- We can confess: *'We are more than conquerors through him who loves us'* (Romans 8:37).
- We can confess: *'There is no wisdom, no insight, no plan that can succeed against the Lord'* (Proverbs 21:30).

We are to use God's word **for** us which is sharper than any two-edged sword, it is living and active.[40] God's word is the sword of the Spirit. We use that to stand against the devil's schemes. God who promised **cannot** lie. We take ground from our enemy, and from 'falsehood', when we use the sword of the Spirit, speaking the truth.

We are also to use our voice to speak up for those who cannot speak for themselves. *'Speak up for those who cannot speak for themselves, for the rights of all who are destitute. Speak* ***up*** *and judge fairly; defend the rights of the poor and needy'* (Proverbs 31:8–9). Sometimes there are people who literally cannot speak for themselves (not just due to oppression and injustice).

The wicked and the oppressor have no such concern about standing up for the rights and privileges of others. We are to ensure those in need receive what is rightfully theirs, and teach them to claim for themselves what belongs to them. We are to speak for every fair, just, and right path. If a person is in Christ, they have an inheritance that can never perish, spoil or fade.[41] This is not dependent on status or 'worldly' standing. They are also co-heirs with Christ.[42] They also have the deposit of the Holy Spirit guaranteeing what is to come.[43] If outside Christ we can show them that God is able to rescue them,[44] and to seat them in heavenly realms. That he will stand by them [45] and fight for their cause.[46] He is able to meet their needs.[47] We are to let our light shine! It is loving to speak the truth. The entrance of God's word brings light.

References

1. 1 John 5:4
2. 1 John 5:4–5; Romans 8:37–39
3. Isaiah 55:11
4. Hebrews 4:12
5. John 17:17; Ephesians 1:13
6. Psalm 119:30
7. John 1:1–2, 14
8. John 1:4; 8:12; 9:5; 12:46
9. Isaiah 55:11
10. John 14:6
11. Acts 4:17
12. Ephesians 6:17; 1 Thessalonians 2:13

13. Luke 21:15
14. John 17:17
15. Ephesians 4:15–16, 29
16. Matthew 12:13
17. Matthew 7:29; 9:8
18. Proverbs 3:25–26
19. Psalm 27:1; Isaiah 41:10; 43:1–4; Luke 12:32
20. Ephesians 4:15–16; Hebrews 4:12
21. John 17:17; Titus 1:2
22. James 1:5–6
23. Romans 8:26–27
24. Psalm 86:7
25. Psalm 55:16
26. Romans 10:13
27. Luke 4:35–36; Matthew 8:30–32
28. Acts 4:29, 31; 5:42; 6:7
29. Romans 8:17, 28; 15:4; 1 Thessalonians 4:16–18; 2 Thessalonians 1:6–10
30. Ephesians 4:15
31. Romans 10:13
32. 2 Thessalonians 2:13–15
33. John 17:17
34. Romans 1:17; Galatians 3:6
35. John 10:3
36. John 12:48–50
37. Proverbs 2:1, 9–10
38. Colossians 4:6; 1 Peter 3:15–16
39. 1 Thessalonians 2:13
40. Hebrews 4:12; Isaiah 55:11; 1 Thessalonians 2:13
41. 1 Peter 1:4
42. Romans 8:17
43. 2 Corinthians 1:21–22; Ephesians 1:13–14
44. Colossians 1:13
45. Psalm 109:31
46. Psalm 72:12
47. Philippians 4:19

Chapter 11

By Our Actions

Letting our light shine by our good works and deeds

'Show me your faith without deeds, and I will show you my faith by what I do. You believe that there is one God. Good! Even the demons believe that – and shudder' (James 2:18–19).

Our God has prepared good works for us to do in advance. *'For we are God's workmanship, created in Christ Jesus to do good works, which **God has prepared in advance for us to do'** (Ephesians 2:10). God **has** made us for good works. There will be a very real and **practical** outworking of our faith. *'What good is it, my brothers, if a man claims to have faith but has no deeds? Can such a faith save him? Suppose a brother or sister is without clothes and daily food. If one of you says to him, "Go, I wish you well . . ." but does nothing about his physical needs, what good is it?'* (James 2:14–16). *'If anyone has material possessions and sees his brother in need but has no pity on him, how can the love of God be in him? . . . let us not love with words or tongue but in action and in truth'* (1 John 3:17–18).

What we do, our actions and our deeds, are important. God's disciples, his elect, his people, will bear much fruit. Showing ourselves to be his disciples. *'This is to my Father's glory, that you bear much fruit, showing yourselves to be my disciples'* (John 15:8). We are to be a people who both hear

God's word and, by faith, put that word into action with a believing and persevering heart.

The **practical** outworking of our faith is important. Jesus will separate people, as sheep and goats by what they have done. The righteous will go to eternal life. *'Take your inheritance, the Kingdom prepared for you since the creation of the world. For I was hungry and you gave me something to eat, I was thirsty and you gave me something to drink, I was a stranger and you invited me in, I needed clothes and you clothed me, I was sick and you looked after me, I was in prison and you came to visit me'* (Matthew 25:34–35). *'Whatever you did for one of the least of these brothers of mine, you did for me'* (Matthew 25:40).

If we really know the Lord, the physical, spiritual and emotional needs of others and meeting their needs (of the Lord), is important.

1. Daily good deeds

We need to persevere doing good and not give up, so we will receive our reward.[1] Daily good deeds include practising hospitality,[2] bringing up children, encouraging, giving, providing for those in need,[3] and for those who ask. *'That our God may count you worthy of his calling, and that by his power he may fulfil every good purpose of yours and **every act** prompted by your faith'* (2 Thessalonians 1:11).[4] *'He defended the cause of the poor and needy, so all went well'* (Jeremiah 22:16). The poor, needy, the outcast, are also made in the image of God, created by him, loved and cared for by him, with the same God-given potential, the enemy has sought to destroy or prevent being released. We are Jesus' body on earth. We will be known by what we do.

God's work is by faith. There is a spiritual element to our daily lives. We are to overcome evil with good. **Those who put God's word into practice daily** have a sure foundation and will not be shaken. *'Therefore everyone who hears these words of mine and puts them into practice is like a wise man who built his house on the rock'* (Matthew 7:24).[5] *'When the storm has swept by, the wicked are gone, but the righteous stand firm forever'* (Proverbs 10:25).

2. A life work

God has also called us to a **life work**. We have all been given specific gifts. God has called us to a unique path. There are often many obstacles to overcome for us to be released into the fullness of the work God has for us. We are to keep persevering until we enter God's plan and purpose for our lives. We are to continue to do good and not to give up. Our enemies will eventually have to submit to us. We are to overcome evil with good. Even when our enemies insult and persecute us, we are to choose to forgive, to love, to keep our heart attitude right. The enemy will **never** succeed in blocking God's plan for us, in walking in the good works he has prepared for us. Our work is to choose to love and keep on forgiving.

We have God's Holy Spirit, we have God's precious promises for us. These enable us to participate in his nature. We have the same power that raised Jesus from the dead working in us. No enemy can prevail against us as we walk according to his will.[6] We have his grace within us, his ability to be faithful, his strength and his enabling. God knows there will often be a battle for right to prevail. *'There is no wisdom, no insight, no plan that can succeed against the Lord'* (Proverbs 21:30).

We need to seek God for his plan and purpose for our lives. We need to hear his voice. He will use our God-given gifts and talents for the good of others: doctor, missionary, evangelist, teacher. We need to hear his call, his voice, and to walk step by step into the plan and purpose he has for each of our lives. We are to keep in step with God's Holy Spirit.[7]

We are to overcome evil with good. God has a plan for us. We are to walk in the good works he has prepared for us (Ephesians 2:10).[8] **Our motive and reasons for doing good will be different from people outside Christ:**

Our good works spring from our love and faith
We don't do good to:
(a) achieve,
(b) get recognition,
(c) satisfy our emotional needs (to feel wanted or to quench our guilty conscience), or

(d)   to earn our salvation.
'For it is by grace you have been saved, through faith – and this is not from yourselves, it is a gift of God – not by works' (Ephesians 2:8).

We give from a place of security. Our strength and ability to stand is dependent on the Lordship of Jesus and our right relationship with him. *'The Lord upholds the righteous'* (Psalm 37:17). We are to put on the full armour of God so we can stand.[9] We are to put our hope, dependence and trust in the Lord. *'Some trust in chariots and some in horses, but we trust in the name of the Lord our God. They are brought to their knees and fall, but we rise up and stand firm'* (Psalm 20:7–8). We need to be:

(a)   secure in the knowledge of God's love for us;

(b)   secure in the knowledge of God's ability to forgive.

We cannot earn or manipulate his favour or others' favour! We are made right with God by faith. From a place of security, of being loved, we are then in a place to act and to give to others. What we do is a consequence of and outworking of our faith. *'Your work produced by faith, your labour prompted by love and your endurance inspired by hope in our Lord Jesus Christ'* (1 Thessalonians 1:3).

We include Jesus

'For it is God who works in you to will and to act according to his good purpose' (Philippians 2:13).[10] It is God's work, we are God's workmanship. It is God who acts and wills in us according to his good purpose. We have God's Holy Spirit within us. *'Unless **the Lord** builds the house, its builders labour in vain'* (Psalm 127:1).

We need a right foundation – God's word for us. God plants his word (from scripture or prophecy) which bears fruit to his glory. God plants in our hearts desires, dreams, ambition, goals that we can choose to fulfil. He instructs us individually in the way we should go[11] (Isaiah 48:17). We need to hear his voice. It is God's work. He will enable us by the strengthening and power of his Holy Spirit. We need to walk in step with God's Holy Spirit into his plan for our lives.

We act in obedience

Jesus' love **for us** motivates us. We act because of the knowledge of God's love and what he has done for us. *'For Christ's love compels us, because we are convinced that one died for all, and therefore all died'* (2 Corinthians 5:14). We love because he first loved us. Loving is to obey God's commands. *'But if anyone obeys his word, God's love is truly made complete in him'* (1 John 2:5).[12] We are to love in 'action and truth'.[13] by our deeds.

What we do is a natural outworking of our faith

We are children of the light.[14] We act as a natural outworking of a life walked, in the light, a Spirit-filled life. *'Live as children of the light (for the fruit of the light consists in all goodness, righteousness and truth)'* (Ephesians 5:8–9). If you make a tree good then the fruit will be good also.[15] *'He who **does** what is right is righteous'* (1 John 3:7).

Our heart-motive is important. We are not to:

(a) aim to please men: *'Am I now trying to win the approval of men, or of God? Or am I trying to please men? If I were still trying to please men, I would not be a servant of Christ'* (Galatians 1:10);

(b) aim for personal gain; or

(c) act out of rivalry.[16]

Our attitude should be like Jesus'.[17] *'But when you give a banquet, invite the poor, the crippled, the lame, the blind, and you will be blessed. Although they cannot repay you, you will be repaid at the resurrection of the righteous'* (Luke 14:13–14). With man this is impossible. *'With God **all** things are possible'* (Matthew 19:26). We have God's Holy Spirit within us. **His** love poured into our hearts. His resources, his great and precious promises. We are to live as servants of God. *'**Whatever** you do, work at it with **all your heart**, as working for the Lord, not for men'* (Colossians 3:23).[18] *'Whatever you did for the least of these brothers of mine, you did for me'* (Matthew 25:40).

To overcome

Ultimately our aim is to be with Jesus for ever in glory. To receive our reward and inheritance, giving glory to God.

3. The use of our money

Money is a gift, a resource. It is a resource, which needs to be channelled for godly goals. God says he will provide richly for us. *'And my God will meet all your needs according to his glorious riches in Christ Jesus'* (Philippians 4:19). He provides for us and more, so we will have enough resources to give to others. *'And God is able to make all grace abound to you, so that in all things at all times, having all that you need, you will abound in every good work'* (2 Corinthians 9:8).

Money is neither our goal nor security. We have a different hope, a different security and a different perspective. We are to put our hope **in God who provides (not in what is provided)**. We know God is the giver of every good and perfect gift. It is he who blesses us.[19]

We are also commanded to do good. *'Command them to do good, **to be rich in good deeds, and to be generous and willing to share**. In this way they will lay up treasure for themselves as a firm foundation for the coming age, so that they may take hold of the life that is truly life'* (1 Timothy 6:18–19).

We are to work so that we can provide for those in need.[20] Work is a means of financial provision. The way in which we both use, and sometimes receive our money, is different from the world. We are to use our money for good and good works, not to build for ourselves a kingdom or to make ourselves feel secure, or to gain power, nor use our money solely for pleasure. Although God does *'richly provide us with everything for enjoyment.'*[21]

We are to:

(a) **Tithe our resources**. God is no man's debtor. He will give back to us. *'Remember this: Whoever sows sparingly will also reap sparingly, and whoever sows generously will also reap generously. Each man should give what he decided in his heart to give, not reluctantly or under compulsion, for God loves a cheerful giver'* (2 Corinthians 9:6–7). *'Bring the whole tithe into the storehouse, that there may be food in my house. Test me in this, says the Lord Almighty, and see if I will not **throw open the floodgates of heaven and pour out so***

much blessing that you will not have room enough for it' (Malachi 3:10).

(b) **We are to give to those in need**. *'Whoever is kind to the needy honours God'* (Proverbs 14:31).[22] *'Be open-handed towards your brothers and towards the poor and needy in your land'* (Deuteronomy 15:11). *'Give to the one who asks you, and do not turn away from the one who wants to borrow from you'* (Matthew 5:42).

We are to *'Give, and it will be given to you. A good measure, pressed down, shaken together and running over, will be poured into your lap'* (Luke 6:38). We are to love in 'action and truth', not just with 'words and tongue'.[23]

(c) **We need to use our money for good works**. *'Command those who are rich in this present world ... to put their hope in God ... Command them to do good, to be rich in good deeds, and to be generous and willing to share'* (1 Timothy 6:17–18).

Our money needs to have been earned honestly. We are not to oppress or plunder the poor.[24] We are not to give poor wages. They need to be right and fair. We are not to fraudulently gain what others have rightly worked for. *'The righteous care about justice for the poor, but the wicked have no such concern'* (Proverbs 29:7).

Some good works cannot be achieved without finances: provision for the poor, the homeless, the fatherless (the orphans). God has those resources for us. We need to ask.[25] They are released as we are obedient in our giving. May *'Our Lord Jesus, that great Shepherd of the sheep, equip you with everything good for doing his will, and may he work in us what is pleasing to him, through Jesus Christ'* (Hebrews 13:21). We need to give so that the Lord can give back to us (see Proverbs 22:9).

We are not to be like the world who hoard their wealth, putting their security in their money, spending their money on pleasure alone, wasting their money on ungodly ventures. They are just storing up wealth for others without realizing![26] We are not to be those who do not trust and believe in God, who in their disobedience take, grasp, and are greedy for self-gain. We are not to store up riches on earth.[27] The Lord is

on the side of those in need, those who have been op
He will see they get justice.[28]

Success, financial success, can be a sign of God's b
(Job 1:1–3).[29] He loves to bless. He loves to give to us, and to
provide for the poor through us. We are his body on earth.
God does provide richly for us. We are not to waste our
resources, our goals need to be righteous.

The Lord speaks clearly about those who are rich in the
world. Having gained their wealth in ungodly ways or on
ungodly projects. We are told that *'a sinners wealth is stored up
for the righteous'* (Proverbs 13:22).[30] *'He who increases his wealth
by exorbitant interest amasses it for another, who will be kind to
the poor'* (Proverbs 28:8). **We need to ask God to release
resources for us, so we can be rich in doing good.** As God's
people we need to learn to give generously, blessing others,
storing up for ourselves riches in heaven.

Letting our light shine by our gifts and talents

False humility is not an asset. It is crippling and disabling. We
were created in the image of God for his glory. **We have
infinite resources in God**. His desire for us is to bear much
fruit, showing ourselves to be his disciples.[31] We have been
given natural gifts and talents for his glory. We belittle our
Creator God when we under-achieve or 'run ourselves down'
verbally. We hurt ourselves. We have also been given spiritual
gifts for the benefit of others.

God has a wonderful plan and purpose for our lives, as new
creations. *'Therefore, if anyone is in Christ, he is a new creation;
the old has gone, the new has come!'* (2 Corinthians 5:17). *'It is
God who works in you to will and to act according to his good
purpose'* (Philippians 2:13).

1. Our natural gifts

(a) For God's glory
A body is *'fearfully and wonderfully made'* (Psalm 139:14). Our
bodies have many and varied skills and abilities:

- **The ability** to read and write (the gift of communication).
- **The ability** of physical activity, to walk, climb and jump, and to excel in these (the gift of movement).
- **The ability** to explore, discover.
- **The ability** to invent.
- **The ability** to create artistically.

We bring glory to our Creator God when we use our gifts. We are made in his image, so when we use our gifts and talents we give him glory, and us pleasure. We are to love God with all our strength, and mind.

Some of these gifts and talents can also be used for the good of others, for therapeutic purposes. We are all able to dance, paint, communicate. Yet some of us are gifted – we literally excel in these areas; in one or more specific area. Our achievement limit is beyond the normal 'natural' ability range. **We have a God-given talent** (all of our abilities are from God). We need to learn to use our gifts to reach our God-given potential.

How will the enemy try to prevent us using our gifts and talents?

It is for God's glory we were created, in his image, to use all our gifts and talents. The enemy will try to prevent us living in the fullness of the purpose God has for us, by:

(a) sickness and disability. The enemy will try to afflict us either physically or emotionally.

(b) undermining our confidence. He will try to undermine our confidence, to try to prevent us achieving. 'I'm useless'; 'I'm a failure'; 'I could never do that'. Lies that cause under-achievement, if accepted.

(c) people actually blocking our path by rejection, discouragement. This may be by parents, others in authority, or colleagues. They do not want you to achieve, to fulfil your potential. They may have a false, wrong dependence or fear (of you succeeding), or they may be jealous, or they may be trying to make you conform to their ideas of the plan for your life!

(d) by withholding finances, trying to block release of finance. This can be very painful when people who we love and care for do not desire what is best for us and oppose us. *'If God is for us, who can be against us?'* (Romans 8:31). God stands with us, as we seek his way and to do his will.

(e) lack of opportunity – given by schooling or parenting – perhaps leading to under-achievement. This may also be due to sin. It is often because of sin people fall short of their God-given potential, and fail to use their gifts, talents and God-given abilities. It grieves God. Unbelief is sin, and the enemy will try to keep us out of relationship with God, the source of our potential.

(f) people who don't know the Lord Jesus and are therefore **out of relationship with their source of potential**, and are cut off from their Creator God, their enabler. We need to be in right relationship with God and with other people, walking in forgiveness, to function at our optimum.

We need to learn to overcome obstacles. *'Everyone born of God overcomes the world. This is the victory that has overcome the world, even our faith. Who is it that has overcome the world? Only he who believes that Jesus is the Son of God'* (1 John 5:4).

(b) For the good of others

God may ask us to use our gifts and talents to enable others, releasing their potential. We may be called to release other people's gifts and talents. This release of gifts is to build up and encourage them in daily life, as well as within the body of Jesus, his Church, *'to prepare God's people for works of service, so that the body of Christ may be built up ... attaining to the whole measure of the fullness of Christ'* (Ephesians 4:12–13).

2. Spiritual giftings

We also have been given gifts of the Spirit. People who are not in relationship with Jesus, do not have these gifts and thereby are not able to release God's enabling, his ability within themselves and others.

God's people have the Holy Spirit within them. God puts *'his Spirit in our hearts'* (2 Corinthians 1:22). We are born again of the Holy Spirit. God's Spirit is a Spirit of truth. This enables us to be led by, and walk in step with God's plan for us. We have the power and enabling of God within us, all his resources. We will bear the fruit of the Holy Spirit.[32] The Holy Spirit enables us to achieve what is humanly impossible because we have God's resources at our disposal. *'He anointed us, set his seal of ownership on us, and put his Spirit in our hearts as a deposit, guaranteeing what is to come'* (2 Corinthians 1:21–22). God is our source of potential. And I will do *'whatever you ask in my name, so that the Son may bring glory to the Father'* (John 14:13–14).

Jesus is the giver of our gifts.[33] We have all been given a gift of faith. We needed that to initially enter the Kingdom of God.[34] We then walk by faith not by sight.[35] We are told to be imitators of those who through faith and perseverance receive what has been promised. *'Imitate those who through faith and patience inherit what has been promised'* (Hebrews 6:12). *'Be imitators of God, therefore, as dearly loved children and live a life of love'* (Ephesians 5:1).

This is how we learn, initially, any skill. We imitate. We need to learn how to use our gifts and talents. Young children imitate, sometimes exactly, adult activities. When we learn to write, we imitate the shape of an already invented letter. Then the skill becomes our own, a learnt skill. We may become proficient, more able than our teacher and go beyond, discovering new ideas, and new skills. Walking by faith is the same. We hear God's word and we act in faith, putting both his written word and prophetic word (his given word for his people) into action. We may have a specific, prophetic word to put into practice. **The more we learn by putting into practice the more skilled we become** with that particular gift or talent. God's work is by faith.

We need to first hear God's word, his call, what he is asking us to do, otherwise there is no vision and without vision *'people cast off restraint'* (Proverbs 29:18), like a ship without a rudder.

We have all been given different gifts[36] within the body as well as different functions. We do not all have the same gifts and talents. If we are an 'eye' we are not called to be a 'foot'. If we are called to be an administrator we are not called to be a pastor. Our gifts are to build others up, to enable us as a body and a people to function and show the fullness of Jesus.[37] His body on earth, reflecting his love and his character.

Spiritual gifts:
(a) **destroy the enemy's work**, setting a person free from the destructive work the enemy has tried to do.
(b) are a **sign to unbelievers** of the reality, presence, and goodness of God.
(c) are the miraculous or the supernatural – the work of God's Holy Spirit, **causing people** to be amazed, and **to ask questions**. By whom and how the miracles are done, and gifts given? It is then that the disciples (and we are) are able to tell them that Jesus worked, *'By faith in the name of Jesus, this man whom you see and know was made strong. It is Jesus' name and the faith that comes through him, that has given complete healing to him'* (Acts 3:16).

Jesus is the author of life. We have a Creator God. The miraculous directs people to Jesus, causes faith to rise. Jesus said, if you don't believe what I say, then believe by what I **do**.[38] What we do is important. We are no longer dead in our transgressions and sin. We have been made alive with Jesus. We have the gift of eternal life. We are relationship with, and have access to, our Creator God. We can ask for gifts.[39] We need to seek and desire our spiritual giftings.

References
1. Hebrews 10:35–36
2. Romans 12:13; 1 Peter 4:9
3. James 2:14–16; 1 John 3:17–18
4. Titus 3:1–2
5. Psalm 15
6. 1 John 2:17
7. Romans 8:14
8. Ephesians 2:10
9. Ephesians 6:11

10. Ephesians 1:11
11. John 10:4–5; Psalm 23:1–3
12. John 14:21, 23
13. 1 John 3:18
14. Ephesians 5:8; 1 Thessalonians 5:5
15. Matthew 7:17–18, 20
16. Philippians 1:17
17. Philippians 2:3–4
18. Ephesians 6:7–8
19. Deuteronomy 28:1–14
20. Ephesians 4:28; Titus 3:14; 2 Thessalonians 3:12
21. 1 Timothy 6:17
22. Deuteronomy 15:4–11; Proverbs 31:20
23. 1 John 3:18
24. Proverbs 22:16, 22–23
25. 1 John 5:14
26. Proverbs 28:8; Ecclesiastes 2:26
27. Matthew 6:19–21
28. Luke 18:6–8; Proverbs 22:22–23; Psalm 109:31; Deuteronomy 15:8–10
29. Proverbs 10:22; Job 42:10–12
30. Ecclesiastes 2:26
31. John 15:7–8
32. Galatians 5:22–23
33. Ephesians 4:8–13; Romans 12:6–8; 1 Corinthians 12:7–11
34. Ephesians 2:8
35. Galatians 2:20
36. 1 Corinthians 12:7–11; Romans 12:6–8; Ephesians 4:9–14
37. Ephesians 1:23; 4:12–13
38. John 14:11
39. 1 Corinthians 12:31; John 14:13–14

Chapter 12

The Importance of Letting Our Light Shine

So, why is it important to let our light shine before men?

1. God will be given glory, acknowledgement and praise

God is the giver of every good and perfect gift. As we choose to use all our God-given gifts, and talents, to our maximum potential, we give glory to our Creator God. This takes credit away from Satan. He gives nothing. He has created nothing. He tries to take, steal, and destroy what God has given us. It is **God** who has created us in his image [1] and given us a multitude of gifts and talents. It is God who has blessed us, forgiven us, and given us a spirit *'of power, and of love and of a sound mind'* (2 Timothy 1:7, KJV). He has made us to be a delight,[2] not only for himself, but for others.

2. They will see God is living and acts on our behalf

God honours those who honour him. He is faithful and just. *'God is just: he will pay back trouble to those who troubled you and give relief to you who are troubled'* (2 Thessalonians 1:6–7).

How will people in the world see God acting on our behalf?

(a) *Our enemies will be seen to be defeated*

'No enemy will subject him to tribute, no wicked men will oppose him' (Psalm 89:22). 'If you listen carefully to what he says and do all that I say, I will be an enemy to your enemies and will oppose those who oppose you' (Exodus 23:22).[3] He will defeat our enemies. 'The Lord will grant that the enemies who rise up against you will be defeated before you' (Deuteronomy 28:7). God is on our side.[4] He stands with us. 'No, in all these things we are more than conquerors through him who loved us. For I am convinced that neither death nor life, neither angels nor demons, neither the present nor the future, nor any powers, neither height nor depth, nor anything else in all creation, will be able to separate us from the love of God that is in Christ Jesus' (Romans 8:37–38). He will not allow the enemy to snatch us from his hand.[5] Nor allow us to be defeated as we walk in obedience to God's will and ways.

(b) *He will vindicate us*

We will be seen to be delivered, if we have been falsely accused or unjustly slandered. It is the Lord who searches our hearts. No action, nothing is hidden from him.[6] He knows all men's motives, as well as our outward actions. 'Because the Sovereign Lord helps me, I will not be disgraced . . . I know I will not be put to shame. He who vindicates me is near. Who then will bring charges against me?' (Isaiah 50:7–8).[7] Those who trust in the Lord will never be put to shame.[8]

(c) *He will see we are given justice*[9]

God's people complained because evil appeared to prosper.[10] The Lord promised that those who still persisted in doing good, who *'feared the Lord'*, that they would again see the distinction between the righteous, and the wicked, between those who serve God, and those who do not.

'Anyone who does wrong will be repaid for his wrong' (Colossians 3:25).[11] The Lord will reward each person according to what they have done.

(d) *We will be seen to be rewarded*

We also have an eternal reward, if we persevere in faith, doing good, pursuing the right course of action. As we set our hearts and minds on **our future hope**. *'Do not throw away your confidence; it will be richly rewarded. You need to persevere, so that when you have done the will of God, you will receive what he has promised'* (Hebrews 10:35–37). *'My reward is with me, and I will give to everyone according to what he has done'* (Revelation 22:12). Our lifestyle, our goals, and ambitions, will change. Our future hope enables us to persevere despite present suffering and trials. People will see we are a different people who know our riches are in Christ Jesus and that we submit to his working.

(e) *People will see the nature and character of our God*

He cares for, and acts on behalf of those in need. God's heart is for the oppressed and the poor, those from whom the enemy has taken.[12] *'Blessed are the meek for they will inherit the earth'* (Matthew 5:5). *'Surely the arm of the Lord is not too short to save, nor his ear too dull to hear?'* (Isaiah 59:1).

People will see the nature and character of Jesus by who we are, and what we do. *'Christ in you, the hope of glory'* (Colossians 1:27). He is a forgiving God,[13] who is able in Jesus, because of the finished work of the cross, to forgive us. Our lives will reflect his desire and ability to forgive.[14]

The world should know we are sons and daughters of the living God reflecting **his** nature and his glory. We are God's workmanship created in Christ Jesus. God's promises for us give us an inner richness, an inner strength. Peter said, *'Silver or gold I do not have, but what I have I give to you. In the name of Jesus Christ of Nazareth, walk.'* That's different! **He knew his authority. He knew his God.** We have the author of life in us.

(f) *They will see God's hand of blessing on our lives*

*'Then all the peoples on earth will see that **you** are called by the name of the Lord, and they will fear you'* (Deuteronomy 28:10).

3. Letting our light shine enables others to be saved

People will know:

(a) **who we are**,

(b) **what we believe**, and

(c) **will see the way in which we live our lives**.

Walking in the light enables others to make informed choices. They can choose to come to a saving knowledge of Jesus. *'Everyone who calls on the name of the Lord will be saved'* (Romans 10:13). *'How then, can they call on the one they have not believed in? And how can they believe in the one of whom they have not heard?'* (Romans 10:14). If people do not know we believe in Jesus, who Jesus is, or what he is able to do, then they are not in a place to make informed choices.

It was because of what the disciples said [15] and did that **people believed upon the name of Jesus**. Peter stood up and addressed the crowd, telling them about Jesus and what they, and he, had done. In response, they asked: *'"What shall we do?" Peter replied: "Repent and be baptised every one of you"'* (Acts 2:37–38). Many people came to a saving knowledge of Jesus, in response to his spoken words. People also saw the miraculous things they did and were told by whom, and how, they were done. *'By faith in the name of Jesus, this man whom you see and know was made strong. It is Jesus' name and the faith that comes through him that has given this complete healing to him, as you can all see'* (Acts 3:16).

This information enabled, and enables, people who respond to be transferred from the kingdom of darkness into the Kingdom of light. [16]

4. Letting our light shine before men gives discernment

It is important both for believers and people in the world that we have insight and discernment, into what is good and bad. [17]

John the Baptist asked, *'Are you the one who was to come, or should we expect someone else?'* (Luke 7:20). Jesus replied to the messengers *'"Go back and report to John **what you have seen**'*

and heard: *The blind receive sight, the lame walk, those who have leprosy are cured, the deaf hear, the dead are raised, and good news is preached to the poor"'* (Luke 7:22).

'*By their fruit you will recognize them. Do people pick grapes from thornbushes, or figs from thistles? Likewise, every good tree bears good fruit, but a bad tree bears bad fruit. A good tree cannot bear bad fruit, and a bad tree cannot bear good fruit ... By their fruit you will recognize them*' (Matthew 7:16–18, 20).

People who do what is right are righteous. '*He who does what is right is righteous, just as he is righteous. He who does what is sinful is of the devil, because the devil has been sinning from the beginning*' (1 John 3:7–8). The reason God appeared was to destroy the devil's work. No-one who is born of God will continue to sin because God's seed remains in him. He cannot go on sinning because he is born of God. This is how we know who the children of God are and who the children of the devil are. '*Anyone who does not do what is right is not a child of God; nor is anyone who does not love his brother*' (1 John 3:10). We are not to judge people. God is the judge. Fruit may take a while to ripen.

5. God's people and God's ways will be seen to work and to prosper

We are a blessed people.[18] We have a loving Creator God **who knows the way,** who has promised to guide us into all truth and to show the way.[19] Jesus said: '*I am the way and the truth and the life*' (John 14:6). '*All the ways of the Lord are loving and faithful for those who keep the demands of his covenant*' (Psalm 25:10).

People will know God's ways are right. '*Then all the peoples on earth will see that you are called by the name of the Lord*' (Deuteronomy 28:10). The enemy will not be able to stand against us, God's Spirit and the wisdom[20] of God. God's word is the truth, they are right, and righteousness.

Jesus grew in stature and **in favour with both God and men.**[21] As we hear and act on God's word, so we will have a firm foundation; good works and fruit will be borne in other people's lives, as well as our own.

6. The devil's work will be destroyed

'The reason the Son of God appeared was to destroy the devil's work' (1 John 3:8). Anything that is darkness is of the enemy. There are *'deeds of darkness'* (Ephesians 5:11). There are people who live in and love darkness. *'Men loved darkness instead of light because their deeds were evil'* (John 3:19). The light exposes and defeats both the men, and the deeds.

Our deeds and our work are of the light.[22] We are part of and live in, the kingdom of the light.[23] *'But whoever lives by the truth comes into the light, so that it may be seen plainly that what he has done has been done through God'* (John 3:21). Light pushes back darkness. God's work is to build, create, affirm, inspire. The work of the kingdom of light,[24] destroys the 'enemy's work': destroys sickness, in body or mind, or anything that sets itself against the knowledge of God. This happens as we speak and walk in the truth. As we bear the fruit of the Spirit. As we have nothing to do with the fruitless deeds of darkness. And, as we overcome evil with good – so light triumphs over the deeds of darkness and the people carrying them out. **Note** the deeds of the enemy, of darkness, are fruit**less**. The enemy destroys.[25] Sin can be forgiven, and the destructive power of sin halted by the saving work of the cross, by the blood of Jesus. His saving grace.[26] We are to push back the enemy, by overcoming deeds of darkness with deeds of light. We are to claim back in Jesus' name, by the power of his Holy Spirit and in his strength, what our enemies have tried to take or destroy, gifts, talents, finances, as well as lives.

In Jesus salvation is found: *'Salvation is found in no-one else, for there is no other name under heaven given to men by which we must be saved'* (Acts 4:12). When someone gets in living relationship with God, accepting and believing in the name of Jesus, asking and accepting his forgiveness, this is the beginning of claiming back what the enemy has tried to steal. It is a mighty victory when someone enters the Kingdom of God. They become light in the Lord. They begin, as they continue to walk in truth and obedience, to bear the fruit of the saints, the Kingdom of light. They themselves instead of being darkness begin to push back the deeds of darkness, in their own lives, and in the lives of others, as well as in the spiritual realm. The fruit of the light consists in all goodness, righteousness and truth.

The light destroys the work of the enemy, who cannot function in the light of God. What we do in obedience to God's word pushes back the enemy:

(a) Every time **we forgive** we get a victory over our enemy. We have overcome bitterness, and hate. This both enables us to enter more fully into God's kingdom, and sets the other person free.

(b) Every time **we speak the truth**, and the truth of God's word, our enemy has to submit to us, and to God's authority. **God's word will accomplish that for which it was sent**. God's word is sharper and more active than any two-edged sword, to heal, encourage, and deliver.

(c) Every time **we put on the armour of God**, we prevent the enemy gaining any ground, in our lives, including being deceived. **We are able to stand** against the devil's schemes.

(d) Every time **we act in accordance with God's will** our enemy is pushed back, defeated. God's whole aim in sending Jesus was to save us from the 'coming wrath', from death, hell and destruction. He did this by sending his Son. Jesus paid the price for us, to be forgiven, to have eternal life, to be with him in glory. As we walk in obedience we secure our place with him in glory. It is those who **do the will of God** that inherit the Kingdom of God.[27] Our safe journey to heaven, having overcome, is our victory, and our reward. We live in Jesus, who has overcome. We will overcome in him. Light triumphs over darkness.

(e) Every time **we pray in accordance with God's will**, we overcome. We are to ask for anything in Jesus' name, bearing much fruit, showing ourselves to be his disciples. *'If you remain in me and my words remain in you, ask* *whatever you wish, and it will be given you. This is to my Father's glory, that you bear much fruit, showing yourselves to be my disciples'* (John 15:7–8).[28]

7. Letting our good deeds, our light, shine before men helps us to stand firm

We will stand firm if we are **walking in the truth** and **speaking the truth**. We will be enabled to stand firm in God's strength by his saving grace, and by his Holy Spirit. *'Now it is God who makes both us and you stand firm in Christ'* (2 Corinthians 1:21).[29] In a sense we are more 'accountable' as others see us and our deeds.

If we acknowledge Jesus in word and in action before men, he will acknowledge us. We will be affirmed. We will reap what we sow. We need to affirm and encourage each other and to be seen to do what is right.

The enemy will be:

(a) less able to trip us up;

(b) less able to deceive us, into believing error;

(c) less able to deceive us that error and wrong doing rewards;

(d) less able to undermine us.

Others will see **their** wrong doing. God's words plainly state God's way, and that the fruit of the Kingdom will be rewarded. The enemy will be paid back for the wrong they have done. *'God is just: he will pay back trouble to those who trouble you and give relief to you who are troubled ... He will punish those who do not know God and do not obey the gospel'* (2 Thessalonians 1:6–7).[30]

*'Do not be deceived: God cannot be mocked. A man reaps what he sows. The one who sows to please his sinful nature, from **that** nature will reap destruction; the one who sows to please the Spirit from the Spirit will reap eternal life'* (Galatians 6:7–8). The enemy will try to entice God's people, trap[31] God's people, tempt God's people to do wrong. A knowledge of God's word is imperative. *'I have hidden your word in my heart that I might not sin against you'* (Psalms 119:11).

8. It will cause our enemies to be ashamed of their slander

People, though they have opposed or slandered us, will see our good works and be ashamed. *'For it is God's will that by doing good you should silence the ignorant talk of foolish men'* (1 Peter 2:15). The Lord does promise to vindicate us.[32] We are to *'Live such good lives among the pagans that, though they accuse you of doing wrong, they may see your good deeds and glorify God'* (1 Peter 2:12). Who we are, the truth and righteousness of what we profess, will be confirmed by what we do.

It is our actions that will speak louder than their slander, misinterpretations, tales or wilful maligning of God's people. *'But whoever lives by the truth comes into the light, so that it may be seen plainly that what he has done has been done through God'* (John 3:21). Jesus said: *'Believe me when I say that I am in the Father and the Father is in me; or at least believe on the evidence of the miracles themselves'* (John 14:11). The world and the people outside Jesus Christ find God's ways difficult to understand, especially in regard to God's grace, his forgiveness. They are far more punitive in their behaviour, less forgiving.

9. Our God-given authority is confirmed

People questioned Jesus' authority, they will question us as well (John 15:20–21).[33]

Jesus **told** a man his sins were forgiven. People questioned both his ability, and authority to do so! So he said: *'Which is easier: to say, "**Your sins are forgiven**," or to say, "Get up and walk"? But that you may know that the Son of Man has authority to forgive sins....'* He said to the paralysed man, *"I tell you, **get up, take your mat and go home**."'* He got up and walked. People will recognize God's authority in our lives. We have God-given authority.[34]

Gamaliel the Pharisee recognized God's authority. *'If their purpose or activity is of human origin, it will fail. But if it is from God, you will not be able to stop these men: you will only find yourselves fighting against God'* (Acts 5:38–39).

10. We will be an encouragement

Others will be encouraged and motivated that those who do what is right, succeed. We all need **daily** encouragement: seeing the good others do, how God has worked for, and through them, encourages us. They encourage us to keep faithful. They encourage us that God is able to keep, to save, to restore, to **win for us** and to overcome. That God is **for** us, and on the side of truth and justice. *'For the eyes of the Lord are on the righteous and his ears attentive to their prayer, but the face of the Lord is against those who do evil'* (1 Peter 3:12). We know that no weapon that is fashioned against us will stand.[35] God's plans, his people who follow and are in step with his Spirit, and his purposes, **will succeed, and be seen to do so**. We have been given abundant life and riches in Christ.

People's faithfulness and obedience to God's work enables us to see and know God's love in action. How much they love God and value others. We are to *'consider how we may spur one another on towards love and good deeds'* (Hebrews 10:24).

11. We will receive honour as opposed to shame and disgrace [36]

Whether people are put to shame and disgrace or are honoured, will depend on:
(a) who they are. We are the children of God and co-heirs with Christ; and
(b) what we do, our good behaviour will secure we are honoured. Humility comes before honour. Pride comes before a fall. Wisdom gives honour. The **fear of the Lord** is the beginning of wisdom.

*'Blessed is the man who fears the Lord, who finds great delight in his commands ... his heart is secure, he will have no fear; in the end he **will look in triumph on his foes**. He **has** scattered abroad his gifts to the poor, his righteousness endures forever; his horn will be lifted high in honour'* (Psalm 112:1, 8–9).

Our enemies will be silenced. It is they who will receive shame and disgrace (Psalm 44:7). We are a blessed people.

Are we going to be a people; a chosen people,[37] who stand up for **truth** and **justice**? A people who say:

- this is **who I am**;[38]
- this is **what I believe**;[39]
- this is **what I stand for**;[40] and
- this is **the way I live**.[41]

According to God's laws of love and his **ways**. *'Blessed are those who have learned to acclaim you, who walk in the light of your presence'* (Psalm 89:15). Are we going to be a people who let our love shine a light? *'By this **all** men will know you **are** my disciples, if you love one another'* (John 13:35).

*'**Whoever loves his brother lives in the light**, and there is nothing in him to make him stumble'* (1 John 2:10).

Are we going to show the way or hide our light under a bush? **Jesus is the way, the truth and the life.**

My heart's desire is that, as God's chosen **people**, beloved and accepted, that Jesus' light would shine through us to those in need, often in desperate need, and to show them the way. And to give glory to our Creator God, who deserves all the credit, honour and praise. We are a blessed people. Is the world going to know?[42]

You are the light.

References

1. Genesis 1:26–28
2. Proverbs 8:31; 12:22; Psalm 16:3
3. Psalm 37:34
4. 2 Timothy 4:16–18
5. John 10:28–29
6. Hebrews 4:13; Matthew 10:26–27; Proverbs 20:27
7. Romans 8:33
8. Romans 10:11; Isaiah 28:16
9. Proverbs 29:26
10. Malachi 3:14–15
11. 2 Thessalonians 1:6; Colossians 3:23–25
12. Isaiah 41:17–20; 42:3–4; Psalm 72:12–14; 107:41–42; 140:12
13. Psalm 103:11–12
14. Colossians 2:13–15
15. Acts 2:14, 34–39; 4:17, 31; 6:7
16. Colossians 1:13; John 12:36; Acts 26:17–18
17. 1 Timothy 5:24–25

18. Ephesians 1:3; Isaiah 61:9
19. John 14:6, 25–26; 16:13
20. Isaiah 54:17; Acts 6:10; 1 Corinthians 1:13–21; 3:18–20
21. Proverbs 16:7
22. Ephesians 5:8–9
23. 1 Peter 2:9–10
24. 2 Timothy 2:24–25; Ephesians 5:11–21
25. John 10:10
26. Ephesians 2:3–8
27. 1 John 2:17; Matthew 7:21–22
28. Matthew 18:18–19; Romans 8:26–27
29. 2 Corinthians 1:21; Romans 14:4
30. 1 Thessalonians 1:6–9
31. Psalm 31:4
32. Luke 20:2; John 15:20–21; Isaiah 50:8–9
33. Luke 20:2; John 15:20–21
34. Luke 10:19–20; Ephesians 1:19–23; Matthew 18:19–20; John 14:12–14; 15:16
35. Isaiah 54:17
36. Isaiah 54:4; 61:7
37. 1 Peter 2:9
38. John 1:12; 1 John 3:1; Romans 8:17; Titus 3:7
39. 1 John 4:2; Philippians 2:6–11; 1 Corinthians 15:3–5
40. Psalm 94:16–17; 109:31; Proverbs 31:8–9
41. Galatians 2:20; Romans 1:17
42. Isaiah 61:9; Deuteronomy 28:8–10, 13; Ephesians 1:3